ESSEX BOY

My story

KIRK NORCROSS

PAN BOOKS

First published 2013 by Sidgwick & Jackson

First published in paperback 2013 by Pan Books
an imprint of Pan Macmillan, a division of Macmillan Publishers Limited
Pan Macmillan, 20 New Wharf Road, London N1 9RR
Basingstoke and Oxford
Associated companies throughout the world
www.panmacmillan.com

ISBN 978-1-4472-4253-6

1 3 5 7 9 8 6 4 2

A CIP catalogue record for this book is available from the British Library.

Typeset by Ellipsis Digital Limited, Glasgow
Printed and bound by CPI Group (UK) Ltd, Croydon, CR0 4YY

Visit www.panmacmillan.com to read more about all our books
and to buy them. You will also find features, author interviews and
news of any author events, and you can sign up for e-newsletters
so that you're always first to hear about our new releases.

Kirk Norcross works as a promoter for the famous Essex nightclub The Sugar Hut. He was one of the founding cast members of Lime Pictures and ITV2's hit show *The Only Way is Essex* and appeared in *Celebrity Big Brother* in January 2012.

To every person who is in, or has lived through,
hard times: this is for you.

CONTENTS

PROLOGUE

Life Now

This morning I woke up alone in my own bed. That is to say, my king-size bed, in my three-bedroom house. I looked at my digital Rolex to see the time, then got up and opened my Louis Vuitton curtains to see the view out towards my dad Mick's massive farmhouse, with its stables, dog kennels and giant fish pond with thousands of pounds' worth of koi carp.

I wandered through to my bathroom and had a shower followed by a session in my private steam room, and sat there thinking how happy I was to be in a house like this. Not many lads of twenty-four could imagine living in the kind of luxury that I was lucky enough to be enjoying.

Then I thought of my mum in her little council flat, and reminded myself that I needed to call round later to see her. She is the most important person in my life, and I needed to be sure that everything was going well for her. I'm now sitting in my office writing this, but later today I'm going to drive to the gym in my white Porsche Cayenne. Until recently I'd have been heading off to film a scene for ITV2 reality show *The Only Way Is Essex*. Then later I might head down to Dad's club, Sugar Hut, and put £1,000 behind the bar to enjoy a few drinks with my mates. Afterwards they will probably come back to mine to play pool in my games room, or watch a film in the cinema room. Not a bad day, is it?! And I still have to pinch myself most days to believe this is my life!

I reckon that is what most people think I do every day. Yes, I do live a pretty privileged life, and I don't hide it – in fact, I am open about the fact that I enjoy it, and that is the life you have seen me live on *TOWIE*.

I'm sure you think I'm a spoilt little rich kid who has been handed money by my dad since the day I was born, grown up with nannies and drivers, and then gone to private school before being handed a job on a plate at Sugar Hut.

Well, the reality is very different. You have to remember that what you have seen on *TOWIE* is only the present. You cannot judge me on my past until you really know it. The truth is, until I was eleven years old and my dad was suddenly wealthy, my idea of a rich person was someone who could afford a school uniform that fitted them, who got a packet of crisps AND a chocolate bar in their lunchbox, and who, if they were proper good all year, got a bike for Christmas.

Even after I realized that there was a whole other level of wealth out there, one where you could own a swimming pool, or fly out to Las Vegas for the weekend just for the hell of it, I never got to experience it for myself until I was eighteen.

Instead my childhood was filled with poverty, homelessness and violent council estates.

The way I see it, there are two sides to Essex. Most people these days know the flash life of Brentwood thanks to *TOWIE*, a place where everyone has money and a nice lifestyle. But don't go assuming that the whole of Essex is like that. Because a world away from Brentwood, across the dividing road of the A13, there is a very different county. Places like Grays and Tilbury are a huge contrast to the glitz and glamour of *TOWIE*. Those towns are poor and run down, and most people live in council housing, struggling to get by. They are tough areas to grow up in, held together by the spirit of the people within those communities, who support one another through the hard lives they are living.

And surprising though it is to everyone who knows me today, this is the Essex that I have seen for most of my life, and has been the biggest influence on me growing up. It is the other side of Essex which has made me who I am today.

ONE

In the Very Beginning

The first thing I remember is sitting in the back of our family car in Asda car park with my older brother, Daniel, when I was only about two years old. Mum and Dad were having an argument outside. They had just finished the food shopping and were loading it into the boot, but as we were watching them shifting the endless plastic bags out of the trolley, their voices started getting louder and louder, and soon they were screaming at each other, both of them mad as anything. Then my mum started crying, so Daniel and I, well, we were confused, so we started crying too. No kid ever wants to see his mum upset. When she saw us she opened the door and threw a 24-pack of crisps in.

'Go on, boys, get stuck in – have as many as you want!' She tried to smile before closing the door again, obviously hoping to distract us and stop us seeing the argument. It didn't work. We left the crisps alone, and just carried on crying and watching Mum and Dad until they were too worn out to shout any more. Eventually they climbed into the car in sulky silence, and we drove home with no one saying a word. I think that's sad, that my very first memory is of my mum and dad rowing, but then I haven't got many memories of them together at all, so maybe it's better than nothing.

My mum, who is called Julie, or Ju for short, and Dad, who was christened Michael but is always called Mick, met and married when they were young, too young to know what they were doing – that's what I reckon now, anyway. They met on a blind date in September 1983 when Mum was seventeen, and Dad was twenty. By then, Dad was a big burly guy with dark hair – although he shaved it off a lot of the time – and Mum was a tiny skinny little thing, with this awful permed dark hair that she started dyeing blonde, and an obsession with shoulder pads. It makes me laugh when I see the pictures, but she promises me it was the fashion at the time.

My mum's mate Maxine was going out with a guy who was mates with Dad, and they set them up. On the second date Dad told her, 'I promise you now, you are going to be the mum of my kids.' Pretty full on, but it didn't take long for that to come true. Just four months later, at the start of 1984, Dad convinced Mum to stop taking the Pill, and within weeks she was pregnant with Daniel. Coming from a strict Catholic family, there was no way Dad was going to let the baby be born out of wedlock, so he told Mum they were getting married, then asked for her dad's permission. From what she told me later, it seems her dad didn't approve, but knowing she was pregnant he thought it was probably her best option. He told her, 'You've made your bed, you can lie in it.'

Because she was still seventeen, Mum's parents had to sign the forms to allow her to marry, so that the banns could be read out. That is how young she was – she was considered by law too young even to decide it by herself!

Then Mum turned eighteen on 4 May, Dad turned twenty-one on 11 May, and a day later, on 12 May 1984, they said their vows to each other in St Thomas of Canterbury Church in Grays, which is in Thurrock, Essex. Mum was Church of England, not Catholic, but she has always felt that all religions are pretty similar, so she was happy to go along with Dad's religious beliefs.

Mum's bump was still so tiny on her wedding day that it hardly showed under her white dress. Both she and Dad were still very young, but I like to think they were actually in love at the time, and that they were going into it really thinking they had a future together. Since then, Mum has told me, 'Kirk, I think it was more infatuation than true love on my part, but I was too young to know the difference,' which is a shame if she is right.

Daniel came along in November of that year, and in the beginning they were a happy little family. But my parents were very different people really. Dad was out working a lot of hours. He has always been a grafter, has Dad. The minute he was allowed to leave school when he was fifteen he was out like a shot. Nothing could have kept him there any longer – education wasn't for him – so he went and got a job. By the time he was married he had decided one job wasn't good enough, so he had two. In the day he was working down at Tilbury Docks, getting stuck into any manual work that was going, and also learning welding, which was considered a pretty skilled job. That was him following in his dad's footsteps.

Dad's family are originally from Blackburn. He was born there and lived there as a kid. But his dad worked on the docks, and had started working in Tilbury, which is on the Thames, staying down south during the week, and going back up north at the weekend. Dad told Daniel and me that when he was five, his dad decided to move the whole family down to Grays in Essex. Later, it had been the obvious thing for my dad to join him working at the docks as soon as he was out of school.

When Dad had finished at the docks for the day, though, he didn't go home to put his feet up – he didn't know the meaning of relaxation! Instead by night my dad worked as a doorman at Hollywood in Romford – a pretty ordinary nightclub that held about 1,500 people, and was really popular at the time, although it is not there any more. It wasn't exactly the best job in the mid-eighties, when there were a lot of drugs around, and things could get pretty rough. But Dad looked the part – he was a 19-stone skinhead, a huge tough-looking guy who could handle himself when he needed to. Not that he was that kind of a doorman – he dressed smartly, and everyone who knew him then has told me he was always very polite, sorting arguments out by talking whenever possible. I think that's why he still has a lot of friends from those days.

Meanwhile, Mum hadn't been a fan of school either. She wasn't the cleverest at academic stuff, and as soon as she could get out, she did. She started working as a carer for elderly and disabled people. Mum wasn't too fussed about a career, though, so as soon as she married my dad she dropped all that, and focused on being a housewife and a mother. She must have thought she was going to be with my dad for ever, so she didn't have a backup plan – she didn't think she would need one. She imagined Dad would always support her financially and emotionally.

On 21 April 1988, when Daniel was three and a half years old, I was born. Here's a fact for you – I share a birthday with Queen Elizabeth II and, more importantly, my Uncle Gary. He is my mum's younger brother, and it was his eighteenth birthday that day, but he was so keen to be an uncle he left his own party to go round to Mum's house to tell her, 'Come on, Julie, get him out of there! I want my nephew out as my eighteenth present, so we can share a birthday.' So she did!

I was born in Orsett Hospital, which is still there although the maternity ward has been knocked down. Mum was on her own throughout the birth, because Dad didn't get the message in time.

I had a pretty complicated birth, as the umbilical cord got wrapped around my neck as I came out, so I couldn't breathe and my brain was starved of oxygen. By the time they had got me free and breathing normally, all the blood vessels in my face had burst from me struggling for breath – I must have looked like a well ugly baby!

The other big thing that happened when I was born was that my mum rejected me. She had wanted a girl so badly –

she'd had a boy with Daniel and was determined she was going to have a little baby girl next. Even when the doctor told her she was expecting a boy, she didn't believe it. 'No, it ain't, I know it's a girl, I don't care what you are saying,' she told him stubbornly. She was so sure she went home and chose a girl's name for me. I was going to be called Emma Louise. Now don't get me wrong, I like that name – if I ever have a daughter that's what I'll call her – but it wasn't right for me . . . obviously!

Instead my dad decided I would be called Kirk John. He liked the name, but Mum didn't. Apparently this is how the conversation went:

Dad: 'Let's call him Kirk.'

Mum: 'Oh no, I don't like that, it's like a dog's name.'

Dad: 'Well, I like it, and so does me mum. She's a fan of Kirk Douglas.'

Mum: 'No, it makes me think of Captain Kirk.'

Dad: 'Well, I like it, and it's my decision, so Kirk it is. Oh, and John as his middle name, as that's my middle name.'

Mum: 'Well, it don't matter anyway, 'cos I am having a girl!'

And that was it settled! Dad definitely held the power. He is a traditional man who thinks men and women have their roles in a relationship, and people shouldn't try to change that. The man earns the money and makes the decisions, while the woman looks after the house and the children.

But anyway, when I came out a boy, my own mum hated me. She had bad post-natal depression and wouldn't touch me, kiss me, go near me, anything. She could not stand me at all. When they let her out of the hospital a couple of nurses even had to come round and feed me and take care of me, as she couldn't bring herself to do anything. Her family all chipped in as well, taking turns at looking after me. After a couple of weeks the doctor told her, 'This is getting bad. You are going to have to start doing something with your baby,' but Mum just shrugged. Dad of course was back at work – there was no way he could take the time off, as we needed the money.

The next day when the nurses came round they decided to let me cry, not deal with me, and see what Mum would do. Apparently I was crying and crying, and wouldn't stop, and the nurses just sat looking out the window, inspecting their nails, doing anything but acknowledge me, until out of pure frustration Mum walked over to me, and everything changed. As she tells it – and I like this version! – 'The minute I saw you that day, that was it, it was unbelievable: I fell in love with you. After that I wouldn't let no one else near you, and told the nurses, "Go on, you can go, I've got this. He's my baby, I'll look after him."' And since then, I've got to give it to her, she really has.

My early months continued to be filled with drama. When I was seven months old, Mum's sisters Tina and Terry were round, when I fell off the sofa and banged my head and had a fit. Apparently I actually stopped breathing and died then and there, and as you can imagine, they were all going crazy, screaming hysterically, and called an ambulance. The emergency services operator gave instructions to Terry on how to give mouth to mouth, which she passed on to Tina, who followed them and saved my life. Obviously I didn't have a clue at the time what was happening, but I am forever grateful to her for that one!

But that wasn't the end of it. From then on I kept having fits, caused by even the lightest touch on my head. So Mum could brush my hair and I'd fit, or I'd shake my head and it would happen, and it was really scary for my mum. I was sent for tests, and it turned out that somehow my fall had caused my skull to be too close to my brain, so if I knocked my head, even lightly, my brain worked by shutting down to protect itself, and fitting. The only way doctors could think of to stop it from happening was to protect my skull until it had grown, so can you believe I had to wear one of those stupid helmets that looked like the headgear that amateur boxers wear. I wore it all the time until my skull developed and the fits stopped. I looked like a proper melt, but at least it got better. I'm just gutted I don't have a picture of the helmet to show you – clearly my parents weren't too proud of me in it either!

At the time we were living at 12 Jesmond Road, in Blackshot, which is in Grays. The area is not the best, but not the worst either. It has little houses and tower blocks of flats, private and council mixed in together, with loads of fields round about. I can't remember the house that well, but it was a small two-bedroom semi-detached bungalow, with my mum and dad in one bedroom, and Daniel and me in the other. I was in a cot first, and then we had bunk beds. I have the impression that although there wasn't a lot of space, it was all nice and homely, and I guess just normal. People would pop in all the time, opening our front door themselves, or coming through the side gate into our little back garden to say hello.

We had a dog, a lurcher called Oscar, and Dad used to take him hare coursing in the fields at the end of the road. There was a lot of space near ours, and although I was too young to go with Dad, sometimes Mum would walk me to the edge of the field where there was a stile you had to climb over to get into it. It always seemed like a huge mountain to get over at the time.

But my favourite thing about that bungalow was the pigeons. Dad had a loft at the end of the garden where he kept the birds, and he used to take them off and race them. It was a hobby of his, and I thought it was great. After he had trained them to use their homing instinct, someone would collect them on a Friday and head off to another part of the country. Then on the Saturday morning the birds would be released, and he would have to sit and wait, and hope they reappeared quickly! I loved the pigeons, and would toddle my way down to the loft and just stare at the birds.

Even now, when I imagine the perfect home that I want for myself, it is a bungalow with a pigeon loft out the back – then I reckon I'd be sorted. I guess that proves it was generally a happy time, the first few years of my life, if a house like that is what I link with happiness in my head.

My memories at that age are all jumbled – just fleeting pictures and impressions that don't always make a lot of sense – but

I do know that my dad isn't in a lot of them. I guess he was working so much it was hard for him to be around. I can't say whether he wanted to see us more but couldn't, or if he was happier out of the house. I do know he wasn't involved in bringing us up much, though, partly because now when we talk about being young, Mum will say, 'I remember the first time I gave you a bath,' or 'You would always do this thing when you were a baby and crying,' or whatever, and Dad never has anything to say like that.

I also know he did have to work hard to keep the money coming in, and even though he was such a grafter, we were always right on the edge of getting by. Dad even had to steal toilet paper from work, as he needed to save money any way he could. It was ridiculous. He would head off to work on a motorbike – Dad has always been a huge fan of motorbikes, and I don't think I have ever known him to be without one – and come back with a couple of toilet rolls in his bag at the end of the day.

Mum and Dad really did start with nothing, and couldn't make ends meet without skimping a lot, but they wanted to slowly but surely build up a life for themselves. Not that us kids were aware of any of this at the time – we just lived in the moment, and that was it. We had no idea if we were rich, poor, whatever!

One of Dad's friends, Chris, told me how Dad had always been ambitious, in a business way, even when he didn't have a penny to his name. He said that to earn money the first winter after they had passed their driving tests, he and Dad decided to ride round in a truck they borrowed from a friend, with a chainsaw, looking for any house where a tree had blown down in the garden or was blocking the driveway. Then they would knock on the door and start bargaining.

'We'll get rid of that fallen tree for you for £20. You won't get a better offer than that now!'

'Oh, I'm sure I can call the council out . . .'

'And how long will that take? It would make a lot more sense for you to use us, madam.'

And inevitably they would get their way, and make some extra cash carrying out fairly standard work – he was working mad, my Dad! So was Chris, who was a bit of an uncle to me over the years. The two of them always had some new scheme or idea. They still do!

One of the few times I can remember my dad being at home with us is as clear as anything in my mind. It's an amazing memory, but also quite scary – and the fact that I can still see even the tiniest details in my mind shows just how much of an impression it made on me.

I was about three years old. Dad came in from work, got changed into a red vest top and gym joggers, lay down on the sofa and pulled Daniel up to sit with him. I was on the floor in front of the sofa, and I still have the picture of them in my mind, looking up at them on this blue sofa with white flecks all over it, Dad with his arm protectively around Daniel. Mum put her head through from the kitchen where she was cooking, and she had a custard tin in her hand – the yellow and blue one with a bird on it, Bird's Custard. Our latest dog, Bella, a short-haired Staffie that my dad had bought recently, was wandering around.

Although Oscar was still alive, sadly he wouldn't last much longer, so it was good that we had Bella already around. She was as soft as anything and I already loved her to bits.

At that moment it was just a really nice family picture. That's how I guess most families are a lot of the time, but it's one of my very few memories of us like that.

But then Dad put a film on the TV. It was *Terminator 2*, which had just come out on video. And, well, I've never been so scared in my life. I watched the whole thing through, literally sat rooted to the spot, too scared even to cry. By the time Mum took me to the toilet before bed, I was hysterical. I was convinced I could see the Terminator next to me, this huge, muscly half-man, half-machine creature, with bits of flesh missing from his face, and metal shining through the gaps in his skin, with his one piercing red eye staring at me. I was crying my eyes out and had nightmares for ages afterwards. Even now it makes me shudder, and I can hardly watch scary films, so nice one, thanks for that, Dad!

We would all watch *Only Fools and Horses* together as well. I didn't really understand the show at the time, but I always associated it with getting milk and Maryland cookies. Mum would give them to Daniel and me as the opening theme tune came on, and we'd all sit there together on the sofa laughing at Del Boy and Rodney. I swear, even now, when I hear that music on TV, I have to go and get myself a glass of milk!

When I was four I started in the infants' class at school. I went to St Thomas of Canterbury, a Catholic primary school on Ward

Avenue in Grays. It was just an ordinary local state school – I don't think there was a private school in our area. No one would have had the money to pay for it, so it would have been pointless.

Dad would drive Daniel and me there in a work van he had by then, most days before he headed off to the docks. There was no school within walking distance of our house, but St Thomas was only a short drive away. Then at the end of the day we would get the bus home with my mum after she'd picked us up.

I was proud of my school uniform when I first got it, especially the stripy blue-and-red tie – it was a good one, that was! We also had to wear a grey jumper and trousers, a white shirt and black shoes. You can see how proud I am in my uniform from the photo of me on my first day at school. They insisted on us being well presented, even at that young age. It was a very religious school – we would have Bible readings and sing from a hymn book before break and at the end of the day.

Daniel and I went to church with Dad most Sundays as well, which I think was a good thing. I even went to classes to get ready for my Holy Communion. I got a real grounding in basic moral ideas and had a religious belief drilled into me from a young age, and I guess that is why I'm still a hundred per cent religious today, although it is not something I talk about much. The way I see it, religion might offer false hope to make people feel better – when you die you'll be fine, you have nothing to worry about and all that – but if someone ends up happier, then who cares? I sometimes think I believe in God partly to make myself feel better about things, but I don't see that as wrong.

So I did start praying when I was a kid, and it is something I have carried on in my life ever since.

As far as school went, I wasn't very interested. I'm not a naturally sociable person, and I wasn't keen to hang out with all these kids I didn't know. Although I try not to let it show these days, I'm pretty shy, and not someone who likes huge groups of people, so school was the wrong environment for me. And I wasn't enthusiastic about the lessons either – I just thought they were boring. I didn't really care about learning to read, or adding numbers together, and besides, it didn't make a lot of sense. It seemed to me that other kids were getting the basics, but mostly I didn't have a clue what the teacher was on about. In those early days I just sat there and put up with it. I was restless, but I stuck it out because I didn't think I had a choice.

While I was still in the infants' class, we moved to a new house. It was a town house at 12 Borley Court, off Welling Road in Orsett, a pretty ordinary village just a few miles down the road from Blackshot. It was a lovely place in a cul-de-sac on a new estate that had just been built – I think we were literally the first to move into the road, which was weird but cool.

It was a tall, thin, brown brick house over three storeys, with a massive kitchen that had a big table in it where we could eat, a toilet and a hallway on the ground floor, with a door from the hall through into the garage, so you didn't even have to go outside to get into your car. On the first floor there was a huge living room and a bathroom, then on the top floor the bedroom I shared with Daniel, my parents' room and a spare box room.

Mum was my whole world, as she was the one who was at home with us. I don't remember Dad being around much at this time. Back then I never questioned how things were, but later on when I was a teenager and thought about it, I resented it. It is only now my thinking has gone full circle – I understand that he was under a lot of pressure to bring in money, so I am back to accepting that is the way it was.

Dad was such a grafter partly because, as I said, he was traditional in his thinking, and took on all the responsibility for keeping the family in money. But then he put himself under extra pressure too. Dad is not the kind of man to just get by in life, or accept a mediocre standard of living for the rest of his years. He wanted our lives to keep improving – which is why we had managed to move from the bungalow to the town house. His attitude was paying off.

I only really have one memory of him in that house. He had ordered a table to be delivered and it had arrived with a scratch on it, and he was arguing with the delivery man, saying, 'I've paid for it, so if it doesn't arrive in perfect condition, of course you're going to take it back and bring me a new one, or I want a refund.'

It's a strange thing to remember, but it pretty much sums up his attitude to money and business, so it makes sense!

What really sticks in my mind from that time is his smell – of the docks, of metal work, and of the warehouse. It's not a dirty smell . . . it's hard to describe, but I guess it is like a grafting man's smell. What you can imagine someone who had spent a hard day welding down at the docks would smell like.

Even these days, if a car mechanic, or someone who works in that kind of job, is near me, the smell from their overalls instantly takes me back to being four-year-old Kirk living in Orsett, running to see my dad when he got in from the docks, before he had had a chance to shower and change, and then head out for his evening's work.

TWO

A Family Divided

After we had been in the house for about six months, and I had
just turned five, my mum and dad had a proper massive row in
the kitchen. And I don't mean the usual kind of argument that
Daniel and I were used to hearing, where they would dig at each
other, shout a bit, then one of them would walk off. This was a
blood-curdling, screaming fight that made us stop playing out
in the corridor and listen in shock. It seemed to go on and on
and on and on . . . We didn't know what to do, so in the end I
think we both started crying!

I don't think Dad ever hit her – he was too much of a gentleman to do that – and she would never have gone for him either,
but this argument really was something else. Later I found out
that she had finally confronted him about a woman called
Stacie who worked at the club, who Mum thought Dad had been
seeing. Apparently she had suspected there was something
between them for some time, but had turned a blind eye. Mum
told me later that when she had questioned Dad on Stacie in

the past, his attitude had been dismissive, along the lines of, 'Go on then, if you think it's true, prove it!' And Mum would just let it go. I don't think she really wanted to know the truth. If she ignored it, she could think that the affair would run its course and Dad would see sense and turn his attention back to her. But this time . . . well, it turned out her brother had spotted Dad and Stacie in a car together, and I guess they were kissing or whatever, and then he had told my mum. So she had to face reality now, and this was the showdown.

The problem was, she gave him an ultimatum – her or the other woman. Maybe she always thought he would choose her, but he didn't. He chose the other woman, so that was it.

'How could you do this to me, you fucking shit! Just get out! I hate you!' she yelled. There was all sorts coming from the kitchen. And it seemed to go on for hours. Then Mum stormed out into the corridor with tears streaming down her face, and said to us, 'You need to go and say goodbye to your dad, boys. He is leaving.'

And somehow, even at five years old, I knew this was serious and we were saying goodbye to him for good. Daniel and I looked at each other and ran into the kitchen, where our dad sat us down.

'Boys,' he said, 'I'm leaving. But don't think you won't see me again – you will. I just have to get myself sorted and then I will come back and see you. Without me here, though, you are the men of the house. It's up to you to behave like grown-up men and look after your mum. Do you promise to do that?'

I stared at him, and nodded, thinking of all the things he

did as the man of the house, and wondering how I was going to be able to do all that. I felt a bit proud as well, though, and determined that I would do a good job, and I stood up a little bit straighter. But then I thought about the fact that he was leaving us, and suddenly it was all just too much.

Daniel was obviously feeling the same. He grabbed Dad's car keys, and we both ran out the front, and my brother threw them down into the drain. I suppose we thought if we could stop him driving he wouldn't be able to leave us. That would be the end of this stupid row, and he would stay, and we could carry on as we were.

But Dad did manage to leave somehow – I can't remember if he got the drain up, or found a spare set of keys – and suddenly that was it. Mum was telling him, 'Go on, go!', and he was getting in the car and going, just these two black plastic bin bags full of his stuff with him – all he was taking away from his life with us. Then he was driving off down the road, and Daniel and I just stood there, staring after him until the car became a dot in the distance and turned out of sight.

Then the crying began. I swear Mum didn't stop crying for about a year after Dad left. It was non-stop, all the time, and Daniel and I just didn't know what to do. She couldn't help it. I think she had proper depression, and I can't blame her – her world had been torn apart. She was still only twenty-five and now found herself all on her own with two kids, no job and no husband. All her future dreams had been shattered. She was allowed to be upset. Fuck, I'd be a total wreck if that happened to me, and I'm a bloke! Mum got married when she was just eighteen, so she was going to be a housewife, grow old with my dad and bring us two boys up – that's all she had in her head. Now she had to find a whole new plan, get a job and make decisions all by herself, but she just wasn't strong enough to cope at that time.

That night I slept in her bed. I don't know if I needed comfort, or if in my new role as one of the men of the house I'd decided it was my job, but I think it reassured both of us. So much so that it became a habit that would continue for the next ten years of my life. I'd go to my mum's bed with her to check she was all right, and then later in the evening when she had stopped crying and gone to sleep, and I was sure she was safe, I would go back to my own bed to sleep. I've never told anyone that – a boy sleeping in his mum's bed until he is a teenager somehow sounds wrong, but from the day my dad left, Mum took on an even more protective role towards us, and I felt like I now had that kind of role for her too. Making sure she slept safely was just one small part of that.

Once I was back in my own bed I wasn't alone either. Bella the Staffie would come and climb in with me, get under the duvet and literally put a paw around me. It was as though she knew something was up and things were changing, and she wanted to reassure me. I swear that dog was like part of the family. I loved her about as much as a sister – if I'd had one!

For me, the first obvious effect of Dad leaving was the way I was with Mum. I'd always been a proper mummy's boy, but as soon as Dad left I got even more clingy around her. I didn't like going to school because it meant leaving her, and I would have all sorts of tantrums to try not to go. I was so dependent on her it was ridiculous. It was like I was still a baby, clinging on to her and wanting her to carry me around with her everywhere. I don't know if it was because I was afraid to lose another parent. I don't know how she put up with it, though!

This was probably one of the reasons why I didn't have a good time at school in those days – Mum couldn't be there with me, so I resented it. Why would I want to be in a building with a load of strangers, when I could be at home with her instead? I also remember that kids in school were always talking about their families and their parents, and it all sounded so lovely and complete. 'Oh, Mummy and Daddy did this with me at the weekend,' 'Mummy and Daddy took me there last night,' – all the kind of stories that just showed me what I was missing. It almost felt like everyone was trying to rub in my face that I didn't have what they had. One time we even had to draw a picture of our families at home, and I didn't know what to do – should I put Dad in the house or not? Mine wasn't this nice complete family like everyone else seemed to have. Mine had just been torn apart.

We didn't see my dad for a bit after he left. He must have been crashing at a friend's or something. But then one day he pulled up alongside the car park near our house where Daniel and I were playing out front, and we ran over. I didn't know what to say to him. Deep down I've always loved him, as he's my dad, but I also felt so much hate for him at that time. Looking back, it scares me how much hatred I had for the man who created me, but all I could think at the time was that he had left me, and, more importantly, he was making Mum feel so much pain.

'How's it going, boys?' he asked. 'I'm going to get myself a place sorted soon, and then you can come over and stay with me for weekends. Would you like that?'

I refused to answer, staring the other way while Daniel chatted happily. He was mature about the whole situation from a young age, and just accepted that our dad wasn't living with us. He didn't feel the anger that I did. Daniel knew that Dad loved him, and was happy to see him, and that was all that mattered. But all I wanted was to make my mum happy – fuck everyone else. I loved her and she was everything to me, so it killed me to see her upset, and I always blamed my dad.

At the end of that first visit he tried to give us some money. He had five pounds for each of us, a note for Daniel and coins for me. When he passed me my share I threw it back at him and yelled, 'I don't want your fucking money!' Even at that age I swore at him – I was so angry. I had heard my parents swearing when they argued, and knew it added an extra force to what I was saying.

He looked shocked but he didn't tell me off. He just said, 'Bye, boys, I'll be back soon, I promise,' and drove off, the money still lying on the ground. Of course once he was out of sight I started picking it up – only to look up and see he had turned the car round the roundabout at the end of the road, and was driving back past, watching me do it. Gutted!

He has since told me that he would do that turn around the

roundabout every visit, just so he could see us one more time. But back then I didn't realize that – I just thought he had caught me out, and I wasn't happy about it!

After that he would pop round now and then, never calling at the house, instead pulling up next to the car park if we were there, to say 'hello'. I'd always go over, but I'd do it moodily, and make it clear I resented him – although I didn't want to miss a chance to see him either, because he was my dad, and I loved him! It was a real mixed-up load of strong emotions for a young kid to deal with.

After a couple of months my dad did get a place, and he came to pick us up one Saturday so we could spend the day with him. Part of me was excited, but another bit of me felt I was letting my mum down. She was crying so much when we left that I felt like a traitor, and nearly didn't go.

This was also when we learned for sure that Dad had left Mum for another woman – we hadn't been told about Stacie at this point. Before we left with Dad, Mum said, 'There might be a woman at Dad's house, the woman he cheated on me with, who I think he is in a relationship with now. Watch out for her, and tell me what she is like, but don't be nice to her – remember what she did to our family!'

And we nodded, confused by the idea that someone could have done that. We could feel the hatred pouring out of Mum as she talked about her. But on that first visit when we pulled up, there was no sign of this other mystery woman, so I stopped thinking about her.

Dad's new place was a one-bedroom flat in a shithole of a place, a real slum of an area in Grays. It was just opposite Seabrooke Rise, which was known as one of the worst estates in Essex. The flat underneath my dad's had all its windows boarded up, as the previous tenant had killed his wife and kids before committing suicide in there. Understandably no one had wanted to live there since.

I was shocked my dad was living in such a horrible place, but I guess he had put all his money into the house we were living in, and he was having to start again with very little. Looking back, I wonder if he had known he was going to split up with Mum one day, so moved us all into a better house before he did it. I like to think he wanted to see us all sorted and settled before he left, which I guess is something I have to give him credit for. Then again, maybe it was as much of a shock to him as to me when he moved out. Maybe he thought he would have been able to see Stacie and stay with Mum and us. I don't know, and really that is Dad's business, not mine.

I don't remember what we did that first visit – I don't think we stayed overnight – but what always sticks in my mind is that as we were leaving, pulling out into the road in the car, a woman with brown hair came walking up and Dad gave her the house keys.

'Dad, who is that?' Daniel asked.

'Just the cleaner, so she needs my keys,' he replied casually, looking straight ahead out the front of the car, and we thought nothing more of it.

But after a few more visits we found out differently. 'The

cleaner' was in the house, and Dad introduced her as Stacie, his new girlfriend. I don't know if he thought we wouldn't remember her from that first visit, but we did. I was so angry. I didn't say anything, but in my head I was shouting at him, 'You liar, that wasn't the cleaner! Mum's right, you really did leave us for another woman. You've just split from Mum, and you're already living with this woman Stacie. I hate you and her!' But I kept it all inside my head and just stood, staring at them all angrily.

We didn't get told it all at the time, but over the years I have pieced together the fact that Dad had met Stacie, who was about eight years younger than him, at the club, Hollywood, where he worked on the door. She worked behind the bar, and at some point their relationship had moved from being co-workers and friends to having an affair, and he must have fallen in love with her.

Of course, from day one I had a real issue with Stacie. In my mind she was the woman who had destroyed my family and hurt my mum, so I was never going to click with her. And I don't think she took to me either. Perhaps she knew I was such a mummy's boy that she would never win me over, so she didn't bother trying. In the beginning we would have conversations, but they were always short and awkward. I wasn't comfortable around her.

Not that we didn't have good times when we went to visit Dad – of course we did. After that first visit we would often stay for the whole weekend, so there was time to do loads more.

I will never forget these mini motorbikes Dad bought for us. We used to ride them around the back yard of the warehouse where he worked down at the docks. There would always be plenty of other workers around – mostly men – but they didn't mind us. They would just say a few nice words and stand and watch us if they were on a break. We were tiny at the time, but I guess it was Dad's way of introducing us to motorbikes, as he loved them so much. Whenever he was driving us there and back through the docks in his van, there was one bit where it looked like the road had dropped away next to us, and he would go really close to it, and pretend he was going to drive us off into the water. We'd be screaming our heads off in the back, genuinely convinced we might fall off. But then as soon as he veered away, we'd be bravely shouting for him to do it again! Other times he took us to a nearby hill and we would go down it on the bikes. I was in the Beavers and so he would also take me to the little hut in Tilbury where we had the weekly meetings, and played games, and whatever else it is you do at Beavers!

Like I said, Dad was always keen for us to go to church, and he kept that up any Sunday we were with him, taking us to St Thomas of Canterbury. And we would also go and visit our grandparents, who lived nearby.

Dad's parents were always very presentable. His dad, Bernard, was always in a shirt and tie, even indoors – I still have a pair of his cufflinks today that he used to wear all the time. He would never talk rude, or think it was OK to fart or burp in front of a lady. He would hold himself well, and always shake my hand. I don't ever remember getting a cuddle off him   it was always a firm handshake, which made me feel very grown-up. He was a real gentleman.

Dad's mum was called Margaret, but I always called her Nanny Pernod, as in the alcohol. Apparently she once bought a dog for one of my uncles – Dad was one of five kids – and he called it Pernod as he liked the smell, and somehow that became my name for her too!

My favourite memory of Nanny Pernod is from when I was very small. Someone in the family had died, but I was too young to go to the funeral, so she was looking after me while everyone else was away. She took me out for the afternoon and bought me a little green stuffed dog that I called Oscar, after the lurcher we had at home. I loved Oscar and took him everywhere, although he was forever falling apart and having to be sewn up, as he got dragged into just about every scrape and adventure with me. He joined my other favourite toy, a car that could play the *Batman* theme tune. That car was great – until I dropped it in a glass of milk and broke it.

When I was about six, Nanny Pernod got cancer of the oesophagus, and had to have her voice box removed and a stoma put in her throat – where they make a hole for you to breathe through instead. It meant she had to have one of those little microphones that you put up to your throat to speak – the ones that make your voice sound robotic. I didn't really understand why she was speaking like that at the time and found it scary at first, and then funny. It was quirky and she used to joke around with it to make us laugh, pretending to be a robot. Ironically, she was cured of the cancer, then a year or two later she was killed by a haemorrhage in her stomach, caused by all the medication she was on. It was my first experience with death and I don't think anyone really told me what had happened, or said, 'She has gone for ever.' I watched her deteriorate, and then she was no longer there. There was a general feeling of sadness, but I only realized she was really gone when I asked, 'Can we go and see Nanny Pernod?' And they said, 'No, we can't.'

Like in my memories of Dad, I associate a smell with Nanny Pernod: the scent of lime, similar to one of those shower gels that smell like real fruit. Sometimes when I'm shopping, I'll go down the health and beauty aisle in the supermarket just for a quick smell of the gel, to remind me of her.

My mum's side of the family were very different. Her parents were called Jean and Fred, although to me they were Nan and Granddad. They were both quite slim and small, and Nan really looked like my mum, just a few years older! While Granddad never went bald, but had this big mass of white hair that everyone always commented on. They lived a couple of miles from us in Tilbury, and because Mum couldn't drive, whenever we went over we had to walk. It was a horrible route along a busy road with no pavement but we had no other choice if we wanted to see them.

Then once we got there, all the men would be telling rude jokes, getting drunk, doing crazy things, even smoking joints on special occasions! Granddad would get someone to roll him a spliff and hide it in with his other rollies, then when he got to smoking that one he'd say, 'Oh, this one tastes a bit different, I wonder why?!'

Nan would shout, 'Fred! What are you doing?!' and he would go off and hide in the shed to finish it without getting in more trouble from his wife. He was brilliant!

It was great fun, and very easy to relax around them, but they were the complete opposite to my dad's parents. We always had to remember whose family we were visiting, so we knew how smart or otherwise we had to be dressed, and how politely we must behave!

Nan and Granddad's house wasn't the only place we had to walk to. It was a pain not having a car where we lived. Because it was a new estate, not many shops had been built nearby yet, so Mum had to walk everywhere – and I mean everywhere. In my memories of her around that time she is always walking, walking, walking . . . She had never taken her driving test for the same reason she hadn't developed a career – she married young and thought Dad would always be around, and as he could drive, that seemed like enough. She would head out to do the weekly shop at Asda while we stayed at home, as it was a hard enough job for her without having to drag us along too. It was quite a mission to get there, but she would head off and reappear a couple of hours later, with dozens of Asda bags all up her arms – she must have had the strongest arms in the world by the time we left Borley Court!

There weren't even any decent bus routes around ours yet that she could use – although that was good for us in one way. Because it was impossible for us to get to school, the council provided a free taxi to and from school for us each day. So actually, we travelled to school in luxury!

But no matter how hard things got on her own, Mum kept on trying. At night she would make a real point of the three of us curling up on the sofa together after dinner, watching TV and cuddling. We always felt really loved by her. And she would do little things to encourage us. She knew I hated school, so she would have some sweets for Daniel and me laid out on the sideboard waiting for us when we got in every day. She always made sure that we got exactly the same amount each. Some days there weren't many, maybe just a couple of sweets, but they were always there as a little reminder she had thought about us during the day. It was one of those things I always looked forward to as a kid.

Mum made sure that we grew up polite, knowing good manners, and to say please and thank you to people. That was her real obsession: 'No matter what, say please when you ask for something, and thank you when you get it!'

And she would teach us good morals as well: to be kind, to share and to help other people. They're basic things, but it can take time to teach them to kids.

Like many single parents, one of Mum's big worries was money. She went back to work after she split up with Dad, which was something she had never expected to do, and brought in money that way. But she wasn't very qualified or experienced, so there was a limit to what she could do. While we were at school she worked in a warehouse, putting leaflets and free gifts inside magazines, and then on Thursday, Friday and Saturday nights she worked in a restaurant, while our grandparents or one of our older cousins babysat. But it wasn't always enough to get us by, and sometimes we would have to turn to Dad. He and Mum didn't have an official agreement about money after he left. Instead he carried on paying the mortgage, and Mum was to deal with the rest of the bills. He would also give her extra money from time to time when she needed help, but he soon stopped that, claiming she was spending it on herself.

There was a lot going on between my parents that we didn't know about, so I can't make too much of a judgement about the way things were. Mum and Dad were protecting us by not telling us everything, and anyway we were too young to understand. But there was one time that sticks in my mind when it was hard not to feel that we could really have used some help from Dad.

The first Christmas after he left, the electricity and gas in our house ran out as there was no money left on the meter. We couldn't believe that they were both gone – and at that time of the year. So Mum called Dad. I don't know what his response was, but for whatever reason we didn't get the money to put in the meter over Christmas. Mum wouldn't have gone to her family about it as she'd have been too proud and didn't want to be seen to be failing. So there we were, the three of us, sitting there on Christmas Day and then Boxing Day, no lights, no heating, no electricity. We couldn't make our Christmas dinner as there was no way to cook, and there was no television or anything like that. We literally just sat there. As the only cash Mum had saved had been spent on food, we hadn't been bought presents, so it wasn't like we had new toys or whatever to play with. I remember my mum crying, I guess because she felt responsible, and it's not what anyone wants for their kids. She must have felt embarrassed, sad and ashamed, but I was just angry for her. She was doing what she could, and then that went and happened. And it was like that for four days. Even having a bath we could only sit in cold water. It was hell, to put it bluntly.

Not that we didn't have happy times in Borley Court. In fact, in a way, that was the happiest time of my childhood after Dad had gone. Daniel and I were closest around this time, mainly because there weren't many other kids our age living on the estate yet. A lot of the houses were still empty so we made do with each other as playmates, and actually, we got on pretty well, despite the three-and-a-half-year age gap.

Like our first house, this one had empty fields nearby, and by now I was old enough to go and roam around them. Daniel and I felt totally free to run wild and created a whole other world for ourselves out there! I swear it was summer most of the time we were living in that house. In nearly every memory I have from Borley Court, the sun is shining and we are outdoors. I am sure we had proper summers when I was a kid, not the 'sun one day, rainy crap the next' that we seem to get these days. And as for the six-week school holiday . . . that went on for ever!

Our favourite place to go was a big field about a minute from the house, which was used as a dumping ground. We would find all sorts in there. Other people's rubbish could be an amazing find for us. Our best discovery was some old office wheelie chairs – we spent hours pushing them to the top of the hill above our house and then racing down. It was great fun – until the day I split my thumb open and Daniel broke his arm. Then we had to stop that one . . .

Other times we would get trays and create sledges to go down these hills in the field that were like mini sand dunes. Or we would make a den behind the bins by the house and entertain ourselves for hours, creating all kinds of imaginary situations, hiding out from our enemies and plotting great military campaigns.

One day we realized that someone had left the key in the patio door of one of the empty houses, so for a couple of weeks we turned that into our own house. The fun lasted until a new family moved in, which was very annoying. Can you imagine – at six and ten years old we were getting on like we owned our own home. It was quality!

My mum's sister, Tina, came to live with us at one point, as she had come out as a lesbian and divorced her husband. She moved into our house along with her girlfriend and two of her kids, Nyanda and Claire, while her son Scott stayed with their dad. Nyanda was around our age and would come out to play with us. We formed a great little trio, as she was just as up for creating adventures as we were – if not more so!

Once, we found a spray can and an axe in the dumping area – I know what you're thinking, and I've no idea why either! – and Nyanda smashed the axe into the can to see what would happen. Unsurprisingly it exploded all over us, and we were covered in purple paint. We tried to get it off but couldn't, so we had to go home. Our mums didn't know whether to laugh or go mad! They practically drowned us in white spirit, and Daniel and I had to have our heads shaved.

We always got so dirty that we had to have baths at the end of every day. When we came home from school, or from out playing, Mum would say, 'Right, kids, straight in the bath before you do anything!' She made sure she kept us as clean as she could.

One day we were walking through the field when a ferret suddenly appeared out of nowhere. It ran up to Claire and was clinging to her leg. She was screaming like anything, so Daniel got hold of a cardboard box and used it to try and pull the ferret off her. It worked in the end and the animal ran away, but I guess that is what you get in a country area, with loads of farms around!

We were a bit obsessed with fires too, which sounds bad, but we weren't pyromaniacs or anything – I think most kids like the power of setting something alight, without really under-standing what the consequences might be. A few times we started fires in the dried grass and straw in the fields, and then watched them burn, quick as anything, until the whole hill was blazing.

Another time someone told us to try spraying deodorant through a lighter to get a really good flame. We sneaked upstairs to give it a go, and Nyanda said to me, 'I'll do it out the window, so we don't get caught! Lean out of the next window and you can watch.'

So I did. But neither of us knew just how big the flame

would be, and suddenly I'd lost half my eyebrows and had singed hair!

We weren't always destructive, though, in case you think that was all my childhood was made up of! The three of us decided to set up a business called Bricks R Us. We would collect bricks from the dump by the house and spend hours writing our names on them, imagining that they would then be ready to sell. Not that we ever did sell any, but the plan was there . . . maybe even then Dad's business talent was filtering down to us, if not very well.

They were probably the best times of my childhood, when Nyanda and her family were living there with us. But eventually they all moved out, and the house seemed really empty. So my mum rented the box room to a builder who was working on new houses on the estate. He lived up north, but stayed down with us during the week. He was fine, but he mostly stayed in his room and didn't have a lot to do with our family. He wasn't much of a replacement for Nyanda! And so life carried on in this way for a while, and we were as happy as we could be without my dad there, while Mum held it all together for the three of us.

THREE

Torn in Two

One day, when I was about seven, Mum told us she was going on holiday to Turkey for two weeks with her mate Lynn. She hadn't been very well with a kidney infection, and the doctor said a fortnight relaxing somewhere warm and away from her usual life would do her good. Obviously we would have loved to go as well, but knew we couldn't afford it, so were happy that she went. She never went on holiday, and she deserved one. We were to go and stay with her brother Gary, which was a bit like a holiday to us anyway, so we were happy with that.

The day she left, she dropped us off, and getting tearful told us, 'Behave yourselves, and remember I love you! I'll be back in no time at all.' And then she headed off.

A few hours later, as we were settling in, my dad came round and started arguing with Gary. We were trying to listen in, but could only make out bits of what was being said.

Dad was telling him, 'I want the kids to come and stay with me.'

And Uncle Gary replied, 'Look, Mick, she's asked me to look after them. They'll be all right here, I like having them round.'

But my dad insisted, 'That's ridiculous. They're my kids, and if she's going to fuck off to Turkey, I want them staying at my house!'

And with that he came and found us, saying, 'Kids, get your stuff and get in the car. You're coming with me.'

We didn't know what to do. We wanted to listen to our dad, but we had been told to stay at our uncle's, and we were happy there. But in the end he was so determined he was right, we went and got our stuff and climbed into his car.

He took us back to his nice two-bedroom house – he had moved twice since first leaving home, each time to a nicer place, as he had been working hard at the docks to build himself back up.

The two weeks passed by without anything major happening. We were at school in the day, and the evenings were just like our usual visits – we played a bit out front, had some food, watched TV and headed to bed. There are just two things that stick in my mind from that fortnight. The first is the packed lunches.

Every day at primary school we would get a packed lunch to take with us. I had never paid too much attention to what other kids had in their little bags or boxes, but mine was pretty much always the same when we were living with Mum. At night she would cook two sausages, and when they had cooled she would cut them in half from one end to the other, and put them inside two slices of bread to make us a sausage sandwich each to take to school the next day. I had always thought that was fine – let's face it, she didn't really have enough food at home to do us dinner each day, let alone a posh packed lunch. She always made sure there was food in us, no matter what it was – she just didn't have the cash for anything complicated. Some nights we ended up with tomato sauce sandwiches for dinner – literally ketchup inside two pieces of bread. But it filled me up, and I knew no different.

So when I opened my lunch that first day staying with Dad, I was pretty taken aback. Inside were cheese and ham sandwiches, a pot of little pieces of chicken, a packet of crisps, a yoghurt, an orange, a carton of juice and a biscuit. I just stared at it – this was like a bloomin' feast! Even my friends who were busy digging in to their own food stopped to admire my lunch – they knew what I usually had, and this was probably the first time ever they wanted to swap with me! I got stuck right in, and made the most of it with a grin on my face. But it was one of the first times I stopped and really thought that things in my house weren't right. And although a lot of the other kids in my area were in a pretty similar situation to us, we really did have less money than my dad, and things you don't think about much, like packed lunches, were a clear sign of that.

The other thing I remember from that fortnight is one of my only really positive memories of Stacie. Dad wasn't very good at helping us with our homework, and I wasn't great at my schoolwork – I always struggled with it. For some reason one night there was one bit of work I really needed to get right

I forget what it was – probably some kind of basic project. The next morning while we were getting ready for school I was crying, as I was worried about the homework.

Stacie came in and said, 'What are you crying for?'

'I have to give my homework in this morning and Dad didn't help me out.'

'Bloody hell, Kirk,' she laughed. 'You should have told me, babe!'

And she sat down with me then and there and we got it done, and then she dropped me off at school and I was able to give it in.

It is the only lovely moment I can remember ever having with Stacie, so it stuck in my mind. I thought to myself, 'If you were like this a bit more, we'd have more chance of actually getting on.'

Then the two weeks finished and carried on into the next, and we realized we were still at Dad's. We started thinking, 'This is weird, where is Mum?' We thought we would be going home by now. But we didn't ask – we didn't ever ask Dad much about Mum as it felt strange to, like we should avoid talking about one parent with the other. Our life with each of them was a secret from the other.

Then, a few days later, I was in the playground at school one lunchtime, and my mum and her friend arrived and came running over.

'Oh, my baby Kirk, I am so sorry! I've been trying to get to you before now, believe me, I have! I would never leave you for longer than I had to,' she said, scooping me into a massive hug, as though we hadn't seen each other in years. She was crying, but I was so happy to see her.

The school let her take Daniel and me out for the afternoon and she explained, 'I have been trying to get you back ever since I came home from holiday, but your dad wouldn't let me. I had to go to the police and everything. He had just taken you, so I had to get the police and the courts and everyone to tell him to give you back.'

Then we walked into Tilbury to the shops, and I was trying to get my head around everything Mum had told us, when suddenly Dad and Stacie pulled up in their car, and well, they weren't happy. 'Kids, come and get in the car. Now!' Dad called out to us.

'Do nothing of the sort!' Mum told us. 'Mick, they're staying with me. Leave us alone!'

And that was it – the whole thing kicked off. Me and Daniel had no idea what to do. It was horrible to watch. They were screaming at each other in the middle of the street, and Dad started sounding a bit aggressive, so Mum told us to go and shut ourselves in a phone box. Everyone in the street had stopped to look, and it just made things worse that Stacie was there.

We ran in the phone box, and in the end Daniel called the police as it just seemed to be getting noisier and scarier. But as soon as we did that, Dad went.

Wow – that whole episode took a bit to sink in! It was weird for me. In a strange way I liked the fact that my dad had tried to keep us. Up until then it had always felt like he was happy to see us, but happy to give us back too, so although I would have chosen to live with my mum over living with him, it was nice to feel like he still wanted us. I understand now that he definitely wanted his kids, but at the time it wasn't the best experience for us.

Our parents should never have been fighting to take us away from one another. The reality was that we needed them both. In my perfect world it would still have been the four of us living together as a family. I'd have killed for that to happen.

I was mad at Dad for another reason, too. When he had first left, he told Daniel and me that we were the men in charge of the house, and that we should look after our mum. So why would he suddenly want to leave her alone without us? She had already lost her husband; she didn't deserve to lose her kids too.

But it was far from over. After that, Dad took Mum to court to fight for custody of us. According to Mum, he told the courts that she was a bad mother and that he wanted us to have more time with him. He claimed she didn't have the money to look after us and she never bought us new clothes. He said when we went to his house we smelt dirty and of cat piss, and that we were getting badly treated. It wasn't true; Mum treated us really well. And like I said, she made us have baths every day. The only reason we might have smelt is because of our clothes. We didn't have a tumble dryer, so getting all the clothes washed and dried wasn't easy for Mum, and I sometimes thought they smelt a bit damp. But that was it. I guess at the time it was turning into a fight between them, so they were bad-mouthing each other. I never heard what Mum said about Dad, but she probably played a lot on him being a bad father who had left the family. I am sure all sorts of dirty tactics were coming out!

Mum told us a man would be coming round to see if we were happy living at home with her. She never referred to him as Social Services, but looking back that is obviously who he worked for. One evening the three of us were curled up on the sofa together, eating our tea and watching television. At the time my favourite shows were *The Queen's Nose* and *Fun House* with Pat Sharp. They were proper good! And we were watching *The Queen's Nose* when there was a knock at the door.

Mum answered and came and sat right back down where she had been before. This guy popped his head round the door and said, 'Hello! And who are you then, boys, and how are you?'

'I'm Kirk. I'm fine.'

'I'm Daniel. I'm good.'

And that was it. He nodded at us, had a quick look around, and then said he had seen enough and left. Mum couldn't believe it. I could see her thinking, 'Is that it? Was that a good thing, or a bad thing, or what?!' It was nowhere near as bad as you would think from the TV. They always make out like Social Services take the kids in for some serious questioning about their parents, but this was so casual I didn't even really notice it happening. He was just a friendly guy visiting our home to see how we were getting on. And although a lot of people get defensive about Social Services visiting, I don't think it's a bad thing – it sounds daft, but if you get a dog from the RSPCA you get your home checked out, so maybe all future parents should be looked at like that. It's weird to think society is more careful about potential dog owners than parents!

Then Mum had to get us new clothes and take pictures of us in them to prove to Social Services that she was getting us what we needed. And all the time, even though I was only seven years old, I was thinking how crazy it was that Mum had to prove to some board somewhere that she was a good parent. How can you really prove that? Surely the biggest thing is love, and we were getting that by the bucketful.

So the man from Social Services wrote up his report and apparently said he didn't see anything Dad had mentioned, but he had seen a loving mum cuddled up to her two kids, and why would someone want to break apart a close family like that? So we stayed with Mum, but afterwards it was made official that we were to see Dad every weekend.

In a way I was annoyed at Dad for trying to get custody, as it had been hard on Mum, but in another way I was secretly pleased that he cared enough to want to see us more. I think it was the bad things he said about Mum that upset me the most. But I'm not a dad myself, so I don't know what passion made him want to fight for us. Maybe in the same situation I'd do anything to see my kids more.

I don't know if my dad would really have wanted full custody, though. I do believe that on some level he wanted us to be with him – we were two boys, and my dad is a proper man, so two boys is his dream. I like to think if he was on his own he'd have wanted to take us in a heartbeat. But my take on it is that my stepmum would not have liked it. And I can't blame her – I wasn't hers, and I could be a right little shit of a kid at times. I hated this woman and I let her know it in the way I ignored her, or was rude to her, so why would she want me there all the time? Dad loved us, and was trying his best, but his priority was Stacie. He didn't want a second failed relationship, so he would have done anything to keep hold of her, believing she was the woman he would grow old with. I did love going to see him, but I never felt at home around Stacie, and I couldn't fully enjoy it. So, for me, staying with Mum was what I wanted anyway.

But we were still struggling financially. The outcome of the custody case was that it was made official how much Dad had to pay and every fortnight his cheque would arrive in the post. Then Mum would get child benefits as well, and any other benefits, depending on whether she was working or not. Dad would sometimes buy things for Daniel and me if we needed them, like a new school uniform or a pair of trainers, but he still wouldn't give extra money directly to Mum, so she struggled to pay all the bills and buy food. It was hard for me to know what was going on. I picked up the odd bit of information at the time, mainly from Mum, and have understood more as I've grown older, but there are always two sides to every story, and it is difficult for me to be sure of the truth. I like to think they were both doing their best, and doing what they thought was right by us – they just had different ideas of how to go about it.

But then all of a sudden, when I had just turned eight, we had to leave our home. Mum would tell you Dad had us kicked out, as he had stopped paying the mortgage after the custody battle. Dad would tell you Mum stopped covering the bills that were hers to pay, and that was the cause. Whatever the reason, the house was sold and we had to leave. We had nowhere else to go.

FOUR

The Anger Inside

Mum tried her best to protect us from the shock of losing our home. She told us, 'Boys, we have to move out of this house. I don't know where we are going to live yet, but we will be together no matter what. And that's what counts, isn't it? That wherever we live, we are all there together.'

We didn't really know what to think. We were quite happy living where we were. In fact the only thing that could have made it better would have been if Dad had come back and lived there with us too. But it was clear from what she was saying that staying wasn't an option, so we just nodded.

It was only later on, when she was crying herself to sleep that night, that she told me, 'Kirk, baby, there's a chance we could end up living on the street. We have no money for anywhere else and your dad won't help me. Please don't worry about it, but I just wanted to be honest with you.'

Inside I was raging at myself. Hadn't Dad told Daniel and me we should be the men of the house now? So why weren't we able to sort this out? There had to be something we could do to make it better. But I couldn't think of a magic answer and it just made me go all angry and sulky.

As moving day got nearer it really seemed like we were going to have to live on the street. The council didn't have anywhere for us, and Mum obviously didn't have the money to pay for a house. But of course Nan and Granddad, Mum's parents, were not going to let us live on the street. Once they realized what kind of situation we were in, they told us to come and live with them until we got ourselves sorted. I think this was a relief to Mum for three reasons. First, obviously, because we wouldn't end up homeless, but also second, because she was struggling so much emotionally with the divorce and being a single mum that it was good for her to have them around as support. Looking back, I think she was probably still suffering from depression.

But the third reason was perhaps the biggest. Mum was born with stones in her kidneys, and she'd had problems with them from the very start. By the time she was eleven years old she'd had most of one kidney removed, and the bit they left behind died. So she has just one kidney, and even that one doesn't always work perfectly. She is prone to infections and even kidney failure, and when that happens, which is about once a year, she can be out of action, in and out of hospital, and even bedridden for months. On top of the pain, it stops her being able to work, which makes her doubly stressed. Throughout her life it always seems to have come at the worst times, and of course it kicked in as we were moving out of Borley Court.

I hate it when my mum has kidney problems. I have always felt so helpless at those times, especially when I was young. I could see she was in pain and I wanted to do something to make it stop, but there wasn't anything I could do.

At least at that time we had our grandparents. They were the caretakers of a secondary school called St Chad's in Tilbury, and their house was linked to the school. It wasn't exactly the best area in the world, but it was friendly, and they had a nice house, even if it wasn't that big. Other than their own bedroom, they just had the one spare room, so the three of us, Mum, Daniel and I, all had to fit in there. I wasn't bothered. I was only eight, and was sleeping with Mum already anyway, so to all bundle into the same bed at night was more of an adventure than a problem. I wasn't old enough to need my own space yet. Daniel, who was eleven by then, was probably starting to find it a bit more difficult, although I don't think it was ever obvious. And as for my mum – well, who knows how she was coping with it.

It worked fine for a while. In fact I liked spending time with Nan and Granddad, so in a way it was like a long holiday. My grandparents were really popular and because of their jobs, everyone knew them. They were like legends around Tilbury! Everyone else called them Nan and Granddad too, and I just accepted that they were all those people's grandparents as well. I'd be walking down the street with my nan, and another kid would pass by, saying, 'All right, Nan Jean?' They all did it. It felt like I had a really big family I didn't know much about!

My grandparents were proper working class, as are the rest of Mum's family. There were no huge successes – it was all very run of the mill, normal day-to-day life. But they were happy like that, and they were always enjoying themselves. Mum's family will just drink, swear, have a laugh and generally enjoy themselves, and make no apology to anyone else for what they get up to. I like that way of living – I always feel comfortable with them, like I don't have to pretend to be anything I'm not.

The area they lived in was very working class too, and a lot of people's hobbies were those of a typical old-school English working man out in the country. As well as things that my dad had been into, like hare coursing and pigeon racing, people were really into horses. There were horses everywhere. People would think nothing of keeping them in their gardens, even if they were living in little council houses, or they would leave them out in open fields and communal areas, just wandering around. There were always horse-drawn carts going around the streets. In most of Britain that is a rare sight, but not in Tilbury, even today. People are horse obsessed! It fascinated me at the time to see them.

Nan was forever baking, and she was really good at it. I loved to sit and watch her come up with some great invention, and after a while, I started joining in. At first I would just be pouring in a bit of flour, stirring, carrying a bowl for her, or whatever – or the best bit, licking the bowl! But after a while I got pretty good at it, and I'd be doing half the work. We turned out some great baking, me and Nan. A vanilla sponge cake is my favourite. I am still a dab hand at making them today!

Other times she would take us into the garden to play tennis, or down to the swings in the park. She might have been a grandmother, but because she had my mum young and then Mum had me young, she can't have been much older than most mums today. So she was still really fit and active and good at looking after us.

As for Granddad, he was a really funny man, always playing tricks on Daniel and me, and teasing us. He would do anything to keep us entertained, and he wanted to make the most of his job to let us boys enjoy ourselves. Of course he was able to do that best during the school holidays. He would open up the school hall, set up all the equipment like the trampolines, the vault and the ropes for us to use, and then invite our other cousins and aunts and uncles to come round too. It was amazing – a whole adventure playground just for us. Then afterwards we would have a barbecue or party back at their house. Those were great days! So mostly, Daniel and I were really happy to be living there. But we were kids, and only had to deal with the ups and downs of our day-to-day existence – not with the harsh realities of adult life.

As for my mum, however, she was still lonely and sad, and felt bad about living off her parents. Because of her kidneys she was on benefits, although she knew she would have to get a job as soon as she got better. So not only were we in my grandparents' house, but they were also paying for our food and all our bills. It really was the only way we could survive at the time.

Mum had applied for a council house for us, but it seemed

like it was a long way off – we were far down some list some-where. She was getting upset about our living arrangement, so in the end her brother Gary, my uncle whose birthday I share, said to her, 'Why don't you all come and live with us for a bit?'

Although he had a wife and two young kids of his own, Gary and his family fitted us into their home. Mum didn't want to impose too much, but they were lovely – they didn't seem to mind us being there at all, and were really helpful. He was also a great emotional support to Mum, and I would see them sitting together late at night, talking things over, Uncle Gary making her laugh.

Then finally, about a year after we had left our family home, the council offered us a house at 81 Hampden Road, in Grays. It was a two-bedroom pebble-dashed house at the end of a ter-raced row, and Daniel and I shared a room, which was fine by me – it was more space than we'd had living with our grand-parents, and we had shared in Borley Court. It wasn't weird in our area to have to share a room with your brother or sister, because most kids were in the same situation as us. In fact there were a lot of troubled children and broken homes around there, so the life we were living was normal.

Mum was working again by now, earning regular money for the first time in a while and paying the landlord each month. She was so determined to make sure he got paid on time, that when he came to collect the rent on a Saturday, if she was at work, she would make sure Nan had the money to cover it and collect the receipt for her.

*

By the time I was nine, I had started to become a bit of a naughty kid, both at home and at school. I was still a real mummy's boy, but I had this weird feeling that is hard to explain, like I was on edge a lot more. It felt like I could never stay still. Even at dinner I couldn't sit quietly at the table – I'd have to walk around the room holding my plate, eating like that. It was as though I had springs inside me that would go off the minute I tried to relax.

At night I would go up to bed and be unable to sleep. I was full of nervous energy – it was like if I stayed in bed a moment more, I would explode. So I would creep downstairs in the middle of the night and do something, anything, that I thought would distract me for a bit, and maybe let me go to sleep later. Most of the time it was just a matter of watching television, something to keep my mind occupied, and after a while I would eventually get sleepy and head up to bed.

Sometimes Mum would hear me, no matter how quiet I tried to be, and would come downstairs to find me. She would sit with me, giving me cuddles and stroking my head, trying to calm my mind down and make me relax.

I'm ashamed to say I also became a lot more aggressive around this time. I would lash out at people for the slightest thing, feeling a real anger growing inside me, then losing my temper so badly I could hardly remember what I was doing, and if anyone got in my way – well, that was it, they would get it.

Mum would tell me off or say something I didn't like, and I would hit her – only a kid's thump, but it was completely out of order. Or I'd hit the walls, or throw things at them – there were holes all over our house because of me. Even as a young kid I could put my fist through the plasterboard. It was pretty shocking behaviour for a nine year old, I admit.

It was only afterwards, when I had got all my anger out, that I would realize what I had done. I'd cry, and say to Mum, 'I'm sorry, I know I done wrong! I didn't mean it, but I didn't know what I was doing. I can't help it!'

And her heart went out to me, and at least it felt like she understood I hadn't meant it. We had such a good bond in that way.

I was a weird mix of contradictions. Sometimes I would be as soft as anything, a real mummy's boy who was polite and sweet. Then other times my naughty side would come out, and I could be anything from cheeky to violent, and have the biggest tantrum ever.

My nan had a way of dealing with it that makes me laugh looking back now. She told me, 'Kirk, I am sick of your tantrums. Next time you want to have one, you go to your room and count to ten. If after that you can still remember why you were so angry, you probably have a good reason to be, so let them have it! But otherwise, behave yourself.'

Sometimes that technique worked, but on the whole it didn't calm me down. And I didn't just keep the bad behaviour at home; occasionally it would come out at school, too.

I still wasn't enjoying school, and it felt like I was falling further and further behind. I really struggled to follow the lessons, and to be honest, I hated being there. I would sit in class and get really angry and frustrated. It was only later on, once I had left school, that I realized I must have dyslexia. It makes so much sense when I think about everything I was struggling with. Plus Mum believes she has it, so that must increase my chances! It is just annoying that no one picked up on it at the time, because it might have made my life in school a bit easier.

I had started to adapt to the social thing a bit more, though, and had a group of friends, but I had developed that defence technique that people have, where they go to the opposite extreme of what they are feeling, and over-compensate to hide the truth. So you know how they say the person who is the most scared in a confrontation is always the first to leap out with his fists up, and go, 'Come on, then, let's have it!' In the same way, rather than let people see I was shy inside, and not confident at all, I would act overly cocky. So at school I developed a bit of a character as a real Jack the lad.

Once a teacher was trying to tell me off and it didn't go down well. I was getting more and more angry, and in the end I picked up a ruler on my desk and hit her, and made her cry. I'm very ashamed of that, but I couldn't take being talked down to. I think the more I felt like I wasn't being the man I was supposed to be – hadn't we had to move house several times because there had been no other option? – the more I was trying to find other ways to prove myself. And listening to authority wasn't on my list of things a man did. You don't tell a grown man off like that, so I thought the teacher shouldn't tell *me* off. Even though I was young, I was starting to flex my muscles in school. I thought nothing of telling a teacher to 'fuck off' the odd time as well, when I was especially frustrated, or wanting people to see me being the man.

I'd based my idea of what a man was very much on my dad, and he was a hard man when he was younger. He had a reputation that meant people wouldn't mess with him, and in the bad area we were growing up in, that was a good thing. People would be like, 'Cor, I know your dad, he is tough!' and I looked up to this geezer for that. So when he told me to be the man of the house, I thought, 'Ooh, he is giving me a role and a face, and if it's like his, I need to be hard. I'm a fucking man!'

I'd have done anything I thought Dad would – I'd have jumped in a fire if it seemed that is what he would have done. And, well, as you can see, I took on that attitude in school as well as at home.

Ironically, it was Dad who was called to deal with me whenever things went wrong at school. I can't remember what I had done the first time it happened, but I was sitting in the teacher's office, and they told me, 'We're sending you home for the day, so we are going to have to get one of your parents to come and pick you up to deal with this. Your mum doesn't drive, so we're calling your dad.'

And sure enough they rang him, and he came and got me. I was shitting myself when I got into the car about what he would say, but he just told me, 'Kirk, I'm disappointed in ya. I was halfway through a meeting and I get called out of it and am having to come and pick you up. The school ringing me up at work like that is embarrassing, I tell ya, so you need to behave from now on!'

And he left it at that. And then we had a good afternoon together! He drove me around the docks and told me about stuff he had done, and pointed things out.

'See that house, Kirk? I built half of that.'

'You like the look of the boat over there, do you? Only in working order 'cos of me, that is.'

And all that. I just stared at everything, proper impressed by Dad. Tilbury Docks is the main port for London, and there is a hell of a lot of stuff to look at: all these huge warehouses, and containers, as well as all sorts of ships docked up, from fairly average boats right up to huge cruise ships. There are people all over the place working away and forklift trucks buzzing around. It is like a little community in itself.

By this time my dad was no longer in overalls – he had started to dress in shirts and smart trousers. He wasn't working on the tools any more, he was now a manager! He had climbed the ranks to work in a company that his dad was a director of, called Grayspur Ltd, also based down on the docks. It was a ship repair and cargo security company that would sort out damaged boats, and build jetties for them to pull up at, and all that, and Dad was a manager.

We stopped off and he spoke to a few people, then as we were driving he kept having to take calls about deals and meetings and all sorts of things that sounded important, even if I didn't understand a word of what he was on about! He was a real businessman, was my dad. I sat there a bit in awe, proud to be with him, thinking, 'Wow, my dad is a real hard worker, a proper man into business and everything. I want to be like that.'

I loved to see him working, but it was weird – it felt as though the new smarter clothes gave him an air of authority, like a lawyer or a policeman, so I was more in awe of him and thought he had to be super successful to be dressing like that.

By the time he dropped me back at Mum's at the end of the afternoon, I had decided I could think of nothing better than being naughty again. Until that day I had never got to spend time with my dad, just me and him, no Stacie, no Daniel, only the two of us. And while I was still confused and hated him, I loved and admired him too, so I wanted that time alone with him so badly, even if I hadn't properly realized it until then.

From then on I decided a telling off from the teacher was worth an afternoon with Dad. Sometimes, just so he didn't get suspicious, I would make out I was ill instead of naughty, and that way he would have a reason to pick me up without it being my fault. So I would play up to that as well. The afternoons I spent with him were the same either way, and I never got bored of them. It really intrigued me. It's just a shame I had to be that bad at school to get to see it!

The other time I did see Dad outside of our weekend visits was on Thursday evenings when I started playing rugby for a local team. He would pick me up and drive me to the playing fields behind the bungalow my parents had been living in when I was born. I must have done OK at the first session, because they asked me to come back and play in a tournament that weekend. I loved playing. I couldn't believe how much pent-up aggression and anger came out on the pitch. It was like, 'What, you want me to be aggressive and go in and tackle the guy? Actually running and slamming into him is not only allowed, it's encouraged? Fair play, count me in!'

But it was only a temporary release, and it wouldn't calm me down beyond the rest of that day. I'd have had to play every day as a professional for that to work! It was good that Dad took me along, though, and it was something we were able to talk about.

Of course I could never tell Mum about the times I enjoyed being with Dad, because it upset her. If I went home saying, 'Oh, I've had the best time!', she'd tell me, 'What are you sticking up for him for? You should hate him, he destroyed our family, ripped it apart!'

But it was especially bad if we mentioned Stacie after a weekend there.

'What did your Dad make you for dinner tonight?'

'Nah, he didn't,' I'd slip up. 'Stacie did, it was good.'

Then straight away she would get the hump. 'Oh, having a good time with her, are ya? Your dad left me for her and you prefer spending time with her?'

I always got what she meant, and why she was upset, but what did she want us to do? I'd sit in my room on my own, thinking, 'Fuck, man, I don't like Stacie for what she did, of course I don't, but I can't help it if she's in my life when I'm at my dad's. I can't ignore her all the time, and refuse to eat her food or whatever, just to keep Mum happy.' It was such a hard place to be in as a kid. I don't blame Mum for being so mad, but I just wish we didn't always have to suffer for it.

All this time Dad's business brain was going into overdrive. Then, sadly, his dad died of cancer in early 1999. He had told my dad after Nanny Pernod died that he didn't think he had anything to live for and, true enough, he soon got sick, and didn't seem to fight it, but just kept deteriorating. He went into hospital for chemotherapy, and lost his hair and put on weight from the treatment. I hated visiting him because the whole place was just so sad and full of death. Ever since then I have had a total hatred and fear of hospitals.

Then he moved out and lived with Dad. I would go round and visit, but he couldn't talk much. It was like he was getting older by the day, right in front of our eyes. I was ten when he died and that fucking hurt. I just wish I had known both him and Nanny Pernod when I was older. I still visit their graves, and talk to them, but I feel like I missed out on a lot of time with them. Partly because of the divorce, I guess, I didn't see them as much as I would have liked. But I hope they are proud of what I have done since – Mum's parents got to see me on TV and I know they were.

I also would like to know if they are proud of Dad, as he achieved a lot of his success after they passed away. Granddad left £500,000 between his five kids. Not bad for a guy who had to provide for five children, as in those days his wife wouldn't have worked to supplement his income. Dad used some of his money to buy a two-bedroom house to rent out, and some to help set up his own company. Now he had moved from welder, to manager, to company director – and he was loving it! Dad is always in his element when he is deep in work and getting results. And getting results he was, in both business ventures

His own company, Delfini, which made signs, built up quite rapidly. If you want to know where the name comes from, my aunt used to work for him as a secretary, and she loved dolphins. Some of their early work was with Greek companies, and the Greek word for dolphins is *delfini*, so they called the company Delfini MB Services – the MB standing for Margaret and Bernard, a nod to Dad's parents.

I remember watching that company grow for Dad. His first office was this shitty little Portakabin on Tilbury Docks, a proper dockers' place, tiny with a load of men in there and porn on the walls. Then he bought another Portakabin and put the two of them together, and then soon after he bought a whole warehouse. It was like you could see his company growing and expanding just by the size of the buildings he was working in, and all this came about because he worked so hard. Metal was his bread and butter, and it seemed to me that he could build just about anything from scratch.

He was also really well respected down on the docks. Whenever I would go with him everyone knew him and would want to speak to him, and they would be good to me just because I was his son. Even today if I go down there, although he no longer has a company on the docks, people will still come over to talk to me, and speak warmly of Dad, and call him 'a proper grafter, one of a kind, your dad'. Which always makes me feel proud of him.

But it was the property that instantly took off for Dad. He hit the market at the perfect time, and started buying and selling houses all over the place, doing some up and selling them on, renting others out . . . and his profits were growing steadily. Not that I was to see any of that for the time being.

When I look back on myself as a ten year old, I feel like I was missing certain things. I don't know if it was because of the timing of my parents' split, but I ended up lacking a few pretty basic social skills. While Mum had done her best to get us ready for the real world, I had developed some habits and fears that she couldn't get out of me, and that she didn't really know how to change. For example, I wouldn't answer the house phone. There was no way I was going to pick that up, when I didn't know who was on the other end of the line. I would get butterflies in my stomach and feel sick just at the thought of it.

And I wasn't happy about eating in public. I felt like people might laugh at the way I ate – not that I had bad table manners – or that I might have a bit of food stuck on the side of my mouth or in my teeth that I didn't know about. It wasn't so bad at school lunches, as everyone was just head down in their lunch boxes, munching away, but anything more intimate, like dinner at a friend's house, was torture. It is only now that I can see this was the start of anxiety, which became so crippling for me later, setting in.

And my schoolwork was so bad that I still couldn't do my

times tables, basic maths, basic spelling or tell the time . . . Plus I was mixing things up a lot when reading or looking at numbers – yet another clear sign that I was dyslexic, but no one seemed to see this.

Deep down I felt like, 'I can't do the work, so I don't want to.' But I was not about to admit I was struggling – instead I would play up and make out like I just didn't want to do it. My entire focus at school was on being the ring leader, the cool kid who would do anything naughty if it got me noticed.

One day I was round at my mate Pete's house after school, just messing about and trying to think of things to do. He disappeared for a minute, then came running back and pushed me out the door. 'Get round the corner!' he whispered, and we sped off before he dived into a bush, pulling me with him.

'I stole a fag off me dad!' he announced, holding out a slightly squashed and misshapen cigarette that he had been gripping in his hand. In the other hand he held a lighter. It had never really occurred to me to smoke before, but there was no way I wasn't going to give this one a go. So we got right into this huge bush on our hands and knees – we didn't care that we were getting dirty – and crawled through into the middle. We didn't want to be seen, although I think we were more afraid of Pete's dad finding out we'd taken his cigarette than we were of being caught smoking!

Pete put the cigarette in his mouth, trying to look all cool, like he had smoked all his life, then he looked at the lighter, confused, before finally taking the cigarette back out.

'What do you do?'

'I dunno,' I had to admit. 'Just smoke it.'

'I don't know how to!' he said, handing me the lighter and putting the cigarette back in his mouth.

I flicked it, and the flame sparked at the end of his cigarette, but it wasn't catching, even though he was blowing and puffing on it.

'No, you need to suck!' I knew that much . . . Well, he did, and straight away he was collapsed on the floor coughing, but trying to pretend like he was fine. Then it was my turn, and I tried not to cough either, even though, mate, it was disgusting. And we worked our way through the whole cigarette, until by the end I thought, 'Oh man, I'm proper dizzy!' but we both agreed that what we had done was a cool thing.

After that, we decided we were smokers, and there was nowhere cooler for us to smoke than in school . . . If anyone needed proof that we were rebels, this was it! So Pete and I, along with two other mates called Ashton and Barry, started scabbing fags whenever we could – from parents, friends, even half a fag off the floor that someone else hadn't smoked, minging though I know that is.

We'd go behind this green container in the grounds of the school to smoke. I've no idea what the container was or did, but it was there. In fact there were green containers all over the place in Essex, come to think of it, in all the parks and that. I guess they were owned by the council. I seemed to spend half my life behind green containers – there definitely aren't enough of them around these days!

So we'd go there for a cigarette in our breaks, and fuck knows, we probably weren't even lighting them properly, or inhaling right, or anything, but we felt like we were, and we convinced ourselves we were.

While we were smoking, there is one thing we used to do that really should have encouraged us to put our heads down and study, so we could go and earn good money when we were older. We used to stand and daydream about a house that backed on to our school grounds. We would look over the fence at this huge white mansion in complete amazement. It was the biggest house in Grays, and we always wondered who lived there. To us it looked like the White House where the President lives in America! We would stand there going, 'Oh my God, imagine living in there. How many millions of pounds do you think the guy living there has?'

'I reckon it must have cost him a billion pounds to buy that. He must be famous, or like a trillionaire. I'll be so rich one day I'll be able to buy one that is even bigger and I'm gonna live in it with my mum!'

'Seriously, though, who does live there?'

But we never spotted the owner, so we never knew.

And then afterwards, when we came out from behind the container, all these girls would say, 'Oh my God, were you just smoking in school? Did you smoke the whole thing?'

'Yeah, we were, and yeah, course I did, man.'

And they'd be like, 'Wow, you are so cool!'

My God, we strutted round there like we were amazing, when the reality was, we were little shits trying to act hard! But that was it, I have smoked ever since. Since that first fag at ten, I haven't stopped.

Sometimes I'd behave myself, and be lovely and polite, and well mannered, making plans and dreams for the future – almost like a sweet little boy! Other times I would be showing off and being the naughty kid. Then at the worst moments something would make me flip, and that was it, I would lash out at anyone around me; I didn't care who they were. No teacher could control me when that happened and the other kids would get scared.

I swear I was like the Incredible Hulk – a bit geeky, a bit quirky, a bit shy and nice, and then bang! Something would set me off and I'd have a tantrum, and you'd have to feel sorry for anyone who got in my way. It was like I didn't know how to deal with anything that upset me. I'd get this huge frustration building up inside me, that would turn into an anger that I had no power to control. Then once I had got rid of it, I would feel horrible and ashamed at the way I had just got on. I never used to cry by that age – it was not a good thing to be seen crying where I grew up – and besides, my dad had told me I had to be a man, and men don't cry. So if I felt like I was going to cry, I'd smash something up instead.

Near the end of year six, when I was eleven, I was in the playground and this girl with plaits turned around and flicked me in the face with them. I was so mad, I went and got some scissors and cut one of them off. She was going nuts, and this boy started defending her, then suddenly six boys were trying to beat me up. I lost it, and really went for them. I beat them as hard as an eleven-year-old boy can. A teacher saw the fight and tried to break it up, but she couldn't, nothing could stop me. Afterwards, when things had calmed down and I was sat slumped in her office worrying about what I had done, she called my mum in for a chat.

She told her, 'I watched Kirk have that fight, and it's not normal for a kid of his age to fight other boys with the complete and utter rage that he had towards them. His temper is really bad, so we would like to see him get some help. It's possible that he has ADHD – Attention Deficit Hyperactivity Disorder – so it might be an idea to go to your local GP and get him to do a test.'

Mum didn't really know what ADHD was, and of course nor did I, so that's what we did, without questioning it. And then the doctor referred me to a kind of social worker who specialized in helping naughty kids and finding out why they behaved the way they did. He asked me what made me upset, and what made me flip, and all sorts of other questions that I didn't know how to answer. I would try my best to explain the way I felt, saying, 'I don't know! I just get the hump if people try and make me feel small, or stupid – I can't just take it on the chin or laugh it off like other people can. I hate being taken for a mug.'

No one took my dad for a mug, so I didn't want them to take me for one either.

They decided that I did have ADHD. Basically, this is a psychiatric disorder that means you are much more hyperactive and impulsive than other kids, and can't focus on things as easily. I'm no scientist, but as far as I can tell they still don't fully understand its causes – although there are certain things that are associated with it. Apparently a lack of oxygen at birth has been linked to developing ADHD as a child, and you'll remember that when I was born the umbilical cord was wrapped around my neck. Suffering something traumatic in your life can help bring it on too, and I guess Mum and Dad splitting up could have been a cause. I was at a really vulnerable age when it happened, and because I didn't know how to deal with that experience, it was coming out in me in a different way to someone who might sit and cry. For me it was showing as this uncontrollable anger.

My diagnosis and treatment were all sorted out over the school summer holiday. I was put on this drug called Ritalin, which is supposed to work by calming you down. At one point my doctor told me I was on the highest dose of it in Thurrock, or something daft like that. Most kids had to take two tablets a day; I had to take five. They were these small white round pills with numbers and codes stamped on them, and I had to have the first two at 8 a.m., then another two at midday, then the last one at 6 p.m.

I also had to go and see this psychotherapist once a week. He was a middle-aged man with a very calm voice. In the first session I didn't want to be there. I hated the stupid questions he was asking, and I lost my temper, saying, 'Mate, I'm not talking to you. What are you going to do about that? I don't want to be here, so fuck off!'

But he just sat back and talked to me, and after a while I

realized he was trying to help me. Even if I didn't want to be there, he had good intentions, so I knew I shouldn't be so harsh on him. And although he didn't change anything for me, I got on better with him after that, and didn't mind going to the sessions. In fact I kept going for the next eighteen months or so, although after a while the frequency of my visits went down from once a week to once a month, to just every now and then, until it was decided I didn't need to go any more.

Mum and Dad had very different reactions to my treatment. I think Mum was slightly relieved that there might be a medical reason for why I behaved the way I did at times, so it was a bit of a weight off her shoulders. But Dad wasn't happy about it at all. He didn't like to think that I had ADHD. He would say, 'It's just a phase. You don't need all this medicine and meetings, you'll get over it in your own time as you grow up.'

The bad side of it all was that I started to feel like taking Ritalin was making me a hard man. I would think, 'This is pretty cool. Yeah, I'm so naughty that no one can control me. I'm so mad I need tablets to control me.'

And the other kids were like, 'Cor, are you on Ritalin? You must be nuts!' and they would be a bit respectful to me because of it, so in a way it made me play up to my reputation.

On top of all this, Mum, Daniel and I had another problem on our plate: we were about to be made homeless again.

After we had been in the house for about 18 months, Mum spoke to the council about her rent, and they said, 'What do you mean, you have been paying the landlord, Julie?'

And she proudly told them, 'Yeah, I pay him bang on time each week, and have never missed a payment, but things are tight, so I was wondering if you could help out more?'

And they told her, 'But Julie, you are not supposed to be paying the landlord anything, that is what we are doing! If you're paying him too, he's getting double the money!'

Wow. That sent Mum into a proper rage. She went straight round to the landlord to try and get her money back, but she didn't have a chance. The guy told her to get lost, and said he wanted us out of the house. I guess he saw it as the easiest way to avoid paying us back, now that there was no way Mum was going to play by his game. We had to move out fast, so Mum spoke to the council, but again they had no houses going spare that they could move us into.

FIVE

Growing Up in a Hostel

So that was it. I was eleven years old and Daniel was fourteen and it looked like we were about to become homeless for the second time in our lives. Not exactly something to boast about.

Mum put her pride aside and spoke to her parents, and we went back to Nan and Granddad's for a while. The three of us in one bedroom. We were so grateful, but we felt like a real burden at the same time. They had their own lives to be getting on with, but now they had to look after us too. And it was embarrassing for Mum – she was thirty-three and back living with her parents. That's not exactly what you plan for your life.

But this time she didn't wait around for someone to come and help us. She was getting wise to this whole housing thing. So she went straight to the council and sat there day after day in their housing department, until finally they told her they had somewhere for us. It wasn't exactly luxury – a room in a hostel – but it was better than nothing. As far as council housing goes, everyone knows a hostel really is the lowest of the low. It's the bottom rung of the ladder, just above homelessness.

Not that I really understood all of this at the time, though – to me it was just another new home, and I didn't really mind. I remember when Mum sat me down on the bed in Granddad's house one day, and explained, 'We're moving to a new home in a hostel. It's a big building with lots of people living in it in different rooms, but at least we will have our own space.' I imagined that it was like going to a holiday camp!

So the day we moved I was pretty excited. A lady called Shelley from the council came and drove us to the hostel in her car. We didn't have much. Any furniture we had owned, Mum had given away, mainly to family, so we put what we had in a few boxes. It was mainly clothes, and bedding, that kind of thing, and we were able to fit that in the car.

The only thing I was sad about was leaving Bella. We couldn't take her to the hostel with us, so she stayed living with Nan and Granddad. They loved her, though, so we knew she would be happy, and we'd get to see her all the time.

Then Shelley took us to the hostel, on Charles Street in the heart of Grays. We pulled up outside and I saw these two three-storey blocks next to each other, with yellowing walls and bars over the windows. It looked like a prison. But that didn't make me any less excited – this was our new home!

Shelley took us through the reception of one of the blocks. We went past a couple of women working behind a desk, and passed what I later found out was the communal living room. Everyone stared as we went by, so I put my head down and stuck close to Mum. We went up to the first floor, where there were ten to fifteen rooms all belonging to different people, and Shelley let us through a door at the end of the corridor.

'Here are your keys,' she said, setting them firmly in Mum's hand. 'I recommend you lock the room any time you are out, even when you go to the bathroom for five minutes, as you never know. There is no security, but any problems, go to reception. Any guests have to sign in there, and this buzzer on the wall means you can let people in when they call you from the entrance to the hostel. The bathroom is down the corridor and you saw the living room. Enjoy!'

And with that she was off, leaving us to explore. The room was smaller than your average living room, and bare, with walls that were supposed to be white but were closer to brown. On the floor was the shittiest, thinnest blue carpet ever, that was frayed at the edges and covered in stains. There was a double bed on one side for my mum to sleep in, and a bunk bed on the other for me and my brother. There was a wardrobe for the three of us to share, but we didn't have a lot of clothes, so we easily fitted all our stuff in there. And, well, that was about it.

Mum was clearly upset and her eyes kept welling up, which confused me. It must have been so hard for her. No one imagines when they have kids that they will be bringing them up in a hostel, and I know that she was forever beating herself up over it. But on that first day she tried to make the most of the situation, pointing out the view from the window, which overlooked a park. I was fine, though – it was our own space, after all. And I was just obsessed with the bunk beds, arguing with Daniel over who was going to get the top one!

Daniel and I went to explore the rest of the building and found the communal lounge, which boasted a television and one sofa with mismatched cushions. And I don't mean the little fluffy scatter ones you put on the sofa, I mean the actual cushions you sit on. It was like the whole thing had been put together from sofas other people had thrown away – which was quite possible. Later, on boring days when I was stuck inside, I would rearrange the cushions to make different patterns, not that it ever made it look better. That sofa was a lost cause.

We also found the bathroom, which contained one bath, one toilet and a couple of sinks, not even a shower. We didn't realize it at first, but we had to share this small bathroom with the whole block – roughly eighty people. You had to queue up to do your teeth in the morning, and everything was dirty and stank. At the time I didn't question it, but now I don't know how we did it. Eighty people sharing a bathroom that was clearly meant for two!

But it still felt like a holiday to me. I thought I was in a chalet at Butlin's or something. I spent the rest of the day running around the place – there were so many corridors to explore and places to hide in, that in a way it was a kid's dream. When we went to bed that night I couldn't stop giggling and being stupid, until Mum snapped, 'For goodness' sake, shut up! Any more and I swear you will be sleeping out in the corridor!'

We quickly found that eating in the hostel was practically impossible. There was never a chance to get into the kitchen and make what you wanted, because someone would always be there first. And even if you did manage to get a spare few minutes, the place was so disgusting it put you right off eating. When I say horrible, I mean really horrible. There was mould all around the kitchen where it had never been washed – it was like you'd get ill just looking at the place. The most Mum ever did in there was bung a pizza on tinfoil and stick it in the oven, all the time avoiding the dried crust of burnt baked beans around the top. Then you had to sit and watch the pizza, to make sure no one nicked it when you weren't looking.

A lot of the time we would skip breakfast, and we ended up living off takeaways later in the day. Not flash Chinese ones, but £1 burgers from the kebab shop around the corner, that kind of thing. Mum would give us the money and send us off to get our tea.

What stopped us existing totally on that kind of food was a friend of my mum's called Maxine. She lived across from the hostel in a proper house. She was there with her two kids, one of whom was my age and I had a laugh with, and I guess you could say they lived a much more normal life than us. But somehow she and my mum were friends, and she was happy for us to go and eat at her house whenever we wanted to. In the end, we would go there most nights. It wasn't anything posh, mostly just chips and beans and things like that, but it was a proper dinner, a nice dinner, and off a clean plate. She also let us use her bath, rather than the stinking dirty one in the hostel. And afterwards we could relax and watch television there too, without worrying someone might hit us in the back of the head for a laugh, or change the channel to what they wanted. My favourite shows by then were *Bernard's Watch* and *Teenage Mutant Ninja Turtles*. Pretty standard viewing for most kids that age.

Maxine really was a lifesaver. It was her and her house that made our time living in the hostel bearable. Not that getting over to her house was the most pleasant walk, despite being only about one minute away! You had to cross this area of grass called Spider Park, and like most parks, it had its resident drunk. This one was called Johnny, and he was a sound old geezer, but he was just too far gone down the booze line to ever fit back into normal society. We kind of knew he was heading towards his death, which was sad, but I'd always say hello as I walked past.

I remember one time I saw his hand out and what looked like his drink spilling, so I went over to tell him to take care.

'Johnny, mate!' I said. 'Your can is tipping all over the . . . oh.'

It wasn't his drink at all. It was just Johnny taking a piss then and there on the bench, not caring in the slightest that I was seeing. But I guess you can't fuss about the niceties of life when you are homeless.

Either way, Johnny was a good reminder that no matter how hard things might have seemed in the hostel, at least we had a roof over our heads; and, more importantly, we had each other. We knew there were always people that bit worse off than us.

Then in September 1999 I was off to secondary school – big school, as we called it. I was going to St Clere's in Stanford-le-

Hope, which is where my brother already went. To get there we had a ten-minute walk to the station, then three stops on the train, then a walk at the other end. It wasn't the easiest, and we always had to make a choice. Dad gave us £10 each a week, and it was £2 a day for the train ticket. So it was a decision. Have lunch and bunk the train. Or pay for the train and not eat. That £2 would get me a lot of food – crisps, chocolate, sweets and a can of fizzy drink, and that was my idea of a good lunch.

The school uniform was another expense for Mum, and once I ripped a pair of trousers scrapping with another kid, too badly for them to be fixed. But Mum couldn't afford to get me new ones until she had been paid. So my brother and I had to take it in turns to wear his trousers and go to school while the other one stayed home. It sounds crazy, but until payday, that was the reality of our lives.

School was getting a little bit better for me now, in terms of my behaviour. It seemed that the Ritalin was actually having an effect on me. The teachers knew I was on it, and I had to have a letter with me at school to say I needed to take the tablets at lunch. It did make a difference. It helped me to concentrate, and I would sit there quietly in class and listen, even if I couldn't do the work. So while I wasn't actually learning a lot more myself, I guess I stopped disturbing everyone else and making the teacher's job harder. I was glad, because I wanted to have a better reputation in my new school. I couldn't be naughty yet because I didn't know the teachers or the other pupils.

There was one big problem with the Ritalin, however. While

it calmed me down – I'd never lash out during the few hours after I'd taken it – it made me bottle my feelings up even more. So then, as the drug started wearing off, my emotions would come out ten times stronger. My poor mum always took the force of it. I'd be fine at school, then it would be wearing off as I got back to the hostel, and then it would all kick off and I'd be going mad until I took my pill at 6 p.m.

We would have huge rows, Mum and me. She has a bit of a quick temper on her too, and we'd lose it, and would go at each other in blood-curdling arguments. Even though I love her to pieces, and did at the time, and she loved me, we were so alike that we were always clashing and then arguing.

The biggest issue was money. It was only once I was at secondary school that I realized why my mum was so upset every day. I began to get embarrassed about where I was living and the fact that we couldn't buy anything.

I understood that where I lived was different when we talked about our homes at school. Daniel had probably felt it before then, but the contrast when I went back to my friends' houses was what made me understand. Don't get me wrong, they weren't in huge mansions, and no one in the area could ever really afford a holiday or whatever – it wasn't that sort of place. But they lived in houses, and could have dinner at night in their own kitchens – that made it special. Mum really wanted to do that for us, but she just wasn't able to. They also had quiet rooms, and tables and desks to do their homework on – not that it would have made a difference for me, as I never did a bit of homework in my life. But if I had wanted to, it would have been pretty difficult in the hostel.

We couldn't even afford to get our hair cut very often, so I always had this stupid long hair that wasn't in a proper style. My fringe would be down to my eyebrows most of the time, and Mum wouldn't let me get it cut until it was right in my eyes and I could hardly see.

Until this time I hadn't worried too much about not having the best of everything, or all the clothes or games that the other kids had. But after starting secondary school these things do matter a lot more. You want to fit in, and have whatever is in fashion, or own something that everyone else is talking about.

I hate telling these stories, because it makes Mum sound bad, and I need to make it clear, she one hundred per cent wasn't. I knew she was trying her hardest, and fuck, man, she wasn't bringing us up badly – she was doing her absolute best. When she could she would get us nice clothes, and she was always teaching us good manners and to keep clean, but at the end of the day we still lived like scum. So even though I would hear her cry herself to sleep every night, I couldn't help asking her for money. I feel bad about it, and I wasn't helping her, but I guess I was just being a typical kid of eleven, and then it would turn into a row.

I'd say, 'Mum, have you got any money? I want to go and buy something.'

'No, Kirk, you know I've got no money!' she'd shout, frustrated at me for asking again.

'Oh, you won't give your son any money. What kind of mum are you? You give me nothing!' I'd kick off.

And she'd start crying, and that would cause a blazing row, and then my temper would be ridiculous and I'd start smashing things up. I'd break stuff.

Some days I'd get really depressed. I'd wake up and feel like I couldn't face the day. Sometimes it was just that I didn't want to have to sit through more school work, or other times it was because of what I didn't have. I know I wasn't the only one in my position – it was the same for a lot of the kids in the area – but I felt so embarrassed if I had to go to school in ankle-swinger trousers because we couldn't afford a new pair. Or things that sound daft now, like everyone wearing one type of shoes, like Rockports, that we couldn't afford. And I'd be there without them, feeling left out. So a lot of the time I would just bunk off. The school would ring Mum, and sometimes people from the council would come and see her, and she would tell me to go. I would for a bit, to keep her happy, but then I'd get sick of it and stay home again. I don't think she really minded, as she knew education wasn't for me and that I was always in trouble anyway. She accepted I wasn't academic and that school was a bit of a waste of time for me. I do feel strongly that school isn't for everyone, and there are different ways of getting on in life. If you aren't academic, it's like torture being there – it's embarrassing.

Instead, I would just be kicking around the park in front of the hostel, because that's where all the kids hung out. Or if it was too cold we'd break into a car and sit in it. We never stole anything, we just wanted somewhere warm to sit, and luckily we never got caught. Until then, I'd never stolen anything in my life. I remember the one time I tried, I took a pack of bubblegum from this shop, walked out, then shit myself and went back in, said, 'Oh, I forgot to pay for these,' and handed over 24p!

I think that was something Mum taught us. She used to say, 'You start stealing anything, you are disowned,' and that was enough to keep us in line. She had her standards and she wanted us to keep to them.

During this time, Mum got a job as a cashier in the supermarket Gateway – now called Somerfield. In our situation that was a good job, and people thought she had done well to get it. If anyone got any job around our way it was seen as well done – there was no snobbery about the kind of work. Especially with Mum's kidney problems still surfacing at times, it was even harder for her than for most. She always made sure we knew how much she cared, and would tell us she loved us every day. Mum also did her best to protect us from the rest of the people in the block, but that wasn't always easy, as there were some right characters . . .

On some levels there was a real communal feeling in the building, like we were all in the shit together, and we'd help each other out, especially among the people who shared our floor. But in another way, there were some proper rough heads that everyone knew as being the ones on drugs, or robbing houses at night. I'd hear people passing the door at 4 a.m., discussing their night's work.

'I got in the back window to that house down King's Avenue. Proper rich ol' geezer lives there, so I done all right tonight!'

'Nice one. Well, if you need to sell any of it, let me know, I've got someone I can right trust at the minute.'

All that kind of chat. And it wasn't just kept to outside of the hostel, sadly. Sometimes people would come back to find their own doors kicked in, and their stuff robbed. Not that most of us had anything worth taking. But I never had a restful night in that place, as we never knew what might happen.

There were kids living in that hostel who were so naughty their parents hated them, and refused to let them live with them, so had kicked them out. Like one guy called Wayne. He was seventeen but had the mental age of a twelve year old, and had been abandoned by his parents as a kid. He was a biggish lad, but was obsessed with the Army, and was always sneaking around the corridors in camouflage clothing, as though he was on a secret mission. Wayne had been in trouble in the past with the police for stalking, and had been accused of rape, although he was never convicted. He used to fancy my mum and would lurk outside our room.

'Your mum in, Kirk?'

'No.'

'Tell her I'm looking for her. I fancy her.'

I never really understood the threat of it, and that it must have been scary for Mum. I just accepted him as another slightly odd neighbour.

The one that freaked me out the most was this guy who, I kid you not, used to walk around in a nappy. He was in his mid-thirties and couldn't talk, and would wander around and just stand in reception for hours on end, staring. It got to me – I was genuinely scared of him. I know it wasn't his fault, as he must have been very ill, but he was like a giant baby – although he never had any nurses with him, or people to look after him. Whenever I was outside and coming in, I'd peer round the door first to see if he was there, and if he was, I'd take a deep breath, psych myself up and – whoosh! – sprint through the door and up the stairs as fast as I could to get past him.

All of this was horrible for Mum. Obviously these weren't the people she wanted to see her kids growing up around, but it was hard for her to stop that happening. One thing she did do for our safety was befriend some of the bad guys, so we would be protected.

There was this big muscly guy called Duncan, about twenty-five years old, who lived underneath us. He was bad news really, a right thief who didn't mind living in the hostel – the way he saw it, he was lucky to be there and not in prison. But Mum got friendly with him and he started looking out for us all. It was like that – you needed people on your side, to make sure things were all right for you. When there are bad boys you want them with you rather than against you. Duncan and his mates started taking over our room, just coming and hanging out there. I loved it, as I felt like I was at the centre of everything, but I could see Mum wasn't happy.

'Come on, lads, we need some sleep now, so do one, please!' she'd try. And they'd nod, but not move from their position, sprawled over her bed, for a few more hours. But this was a small price to pay for their protection.

As for Dad, our visits had dropped from every weekend to every other weekend. Looking back, I think he wanted to spend time with his kids, but was torn between us and Stacie. At the time, though, it seemed like Dad wasn't really interested in us. If we were lucky he took us to the park for a kick-about, or to the cinema, but a lot of the time we were just left to entertain ourselves.

My relationship with Stacie had reached an all-time low. I could just about make myself say 'hello' to her when we arrived, and that was it. I felt as if she didn't want us there, and nor, it seemed, did Dad. I saw the whole visit as a waste of time.

I also hated the pain it still caused Mum when we went to stay with Dad. She'd try to hide it at first when we got back, sulking but not saying why. Then it would come out in an outburst, which could be caused by anything. Like she'd say, 'Come on, then, time for dinner.'

And without thinking, I'd reply, 'No, we're all right, we had a massive lunch at Dad's, so I'm not hungry.'

'Oh, you prefer to eat with your dad, do you? Oh right, I get it. And I suppose her, too. Like your new mum, is she? Love her now, do you?'

And it would go on and on. It caused so much grief, I'd rather not have gone round to Dad's in the first place.

Another time my brother was going on a school trip to some museum and he was so excited about it. The day before we went round to Dad's, and Stacie fancied herself as a bit of a hair-dresser, so she cut Daniel's hair. When we got home, Mum was so pissed off that he had let her do it, she said, 'Look at the state of you, you let that cow cut your hair! Right, sit down here. I'll make it better!' and she took chunks out of his hair with clippers. He looked a right state and was crying his eyes out and had to go on this school trip the next day looking like he'd had a fight with a lawnmower.

I didn't blame Mum on one level – what Dad had put her through was horrible. And I'm sure she sat there when we were away for the weekend imagining us all playing happy families without her, even though that's not how it was at all. Dad did sometimes ask Daniel and me to go and live with him, but it was like he felt he had to say it, as we were his kids by blood, rather than because he really wanted us to live there. We didn't want to anyway, and we'd never have done that to Mum. I honestly believe if we had left her, she'd have killed herself.

I still have never understood why Dad didn't help Mum out more. I'm sure he had his reasons, but after we said we were staying with Mum, I wish he had said, 'Right, if that's the path you're taking, I'll buy your mum a house.'

If it was me in his position, I would work double the amount, I'd work my fingers to the bone for my family, to do whatever it took to get them out of a hostel. But he didn't, and I do think that is sad.

I think he must have felt caught as he obviously had commitments to Stacie as well, so it wasn't just up to him what he did.

Christmas was no better. We'd spend it with Mum one year and with Dad the next, and Christmas 1999 it was Dad's turn to have us. Mum spent the whole lead-up through December crying her eyes out every day. She would say, 'I can't afford to get you presents. What kind of a mum am I?'

And I'd tell her, 'Mum, don't worry, we don't want presents!'

But of course I did. What kid doesn't? And she saved up and got me a Michael Jackson cassette, and my brother a video. I knew presents were where Dad could excel, though. So even though Christmas itself was rubbish, as Dad and Stacie rowed all day, the food was good, and Dad wasn't bad for a Game Boy or new clothes.

I tried to hide them back at the hostel, and make out like Dad had hardly given us much, but when Mum did see the presents you could see the pain in her eyes, like it was killing her, and I wished I'd never even been given anything at all.

One weekend in the spring of 2000, Dad told us, 'I'm gonna be moving house, boys – not far, I'll still be in Grays, but I've been saving my money lately and me and Stacie are going to be in a nicer house.'

Well, it didn't mean too much to us at first. He was still in the area, and as we didn't live there it just meant there was a different house to visit. But then it got to the next week and he gave us the address and we headed over to see him. As we got closer, it dawned on us which house it was. Only the huge white one by my primary school that I used to dream of living in, the biggest bloody house in the town! Daniel and I couldn't believe it. Had he won the Lottery or something?!

I'm not lying, it reminded me of that house in *The Fresh Prince of Bel-Air*, when you see the outside of it with Jazzy Jeff being thrown out the door all the time. It was huge. I went crazy running round exploring it, and Dad was showing us everything, trying to hide how proud he was, but his voice gave it away. There was a library, a gym, a dance floor, a snooker room, and a garage complex with another flat on top where he let one of his brothers live. And inside the garage even his car had changed. Where Dad used to drive a Golf GTI, a normal car that teenagers would drive, suddenly he now had a new Mercedes. So new, in fact, that he wasn't even allowed to drive it on English roads. It was like, what the fuck?! How the hell did he have all this money overnight?

He explained, 'I've been saving over the last few years, boys, and not spending. Where most people spend what they earn, no matter what it is, I have been sensible, and it has paid off. I've not spent out on stupid things and spoilt myself, and this is the result, I am able to do this. Remember that for your future, boys!'

And it did make an impression. We knew he had worked his arse off all his life, and to see it coming to something was amazing. Daniel and I both listened and took it in. And of course we couldn't help but compare it with where we were living with our mum. It was such a world away. We only walked ten minutes up a hill to reach Dad's house, but it was like coming to a different planet. We'd leave this hostel where our whole life was in one room, walk past a fourteen year old in the corridor trying to deal with a crying baby, dodge a slap from one of the older druggies, and pass drunken Johnny on the bench. Walk up the hill, and bam, suddenly we were at Dad's house, the biggest and best house in Grays! A house for three people that was bigger than our hostel for eighty. Where is the sense in that?

How could my parents, once married and living together, now be living such completely different lives? That's when reality hit home, and stopped us being totally happy about Dad's new place. I thought, 'Fuck, man, this doesn't seem right.'

So I said to him, 'We're not happy at home, Dad. Mum needs money, can you please help her out?'

But he shook his head and said, 'Well, come and live with us. You know you can, any time you want.'

But I told him, 'No way, I can't. Well, it's not that I couldn't, but I don't want to. There's no way I'm going to leave my mum.'

And it was true, there was no way I was going to do that. I didn't care if we ended up in the street living in a cardboard box – even then if my dad told me to go and live with him, I'd still stay in the box with my mum. At the end of the day it was him who left her, and I watched her suffer for it, trying to be a good parent and doing everything for me. I would never have left her as our bond was more important than money. No matter what has happened in my life, whether I've had money or not, I never let myself forget that.

And actually, while I loved visiting that house of Dad's – who wouldn't? – I never felt like it was my home. I always felt like a guest. 'Please can I go to the toilet, Dad?' It was as ridiculous as that, and it was clear it was Stacie's house and not ours. My relationship with her, which was never good, had been on a steady downward slope over the years, and our awkward conversations were no longer that. They had been replaced by us ignoring each other, or arguing.

One of my biggest problems with her is that she would have digs at my mum when she was talking to Dad. I know that's probably normal in this situation, but I just wasn't willing to take it. She would say things like, 'Look at the state of the boys' clothes. Their mum clearly doesn't look after them.'

And I'd be standing there fuming with the rage building, until I'd explode, 'Oi, shut up you, this is my mum you are talking about!'

But then because he was so protective of Stacie and never let me talk badly to her, Dad would tell me, 'That's enough, don't talk to Stacie like that. Shut it!'

And I would be even more angry in my head, going, 'Fucking hell, don't talk about my mum like that in front of me! And as for you, Dad, you won't even let me stick up for her!'

I was convinced in my young mind that Stacie had gone for Dad in some kind of a weird vendetta against my family, like she had fallen for him on purpose. Why else would you get together with a married man? It's only now I'm older I know you can't help who you fall in love with. It can't have been an ideal situation for her either. 'Oh, you know what, I want to go out and find a happily married man, destroy his family and get him for myself, then have to take on his angry little kids as well.'

91

It obviously wasn't her aim. But at the same time, I think she should have had more willpower when they first met, and thought, 'Actually, he has a wife – I'll back off.' But then so should Dad. He was the one who had made vows to Mum to stay with her for ever, and then failed to do that so soon after, despite his strict Catholic views. Ugh, it's so hard, and it makes me angry thinking over it again as I'm writing this. You can see I go round in circles about it! Over the years I have gone through it so many times my brain hurts. I think the truth is that I'm never going to be OK with it, really.

The thing that hurts, that makes me so resentful and stops me getting past it, is that I always think how different my childhood could have been, and how much better a life my mum could have had.

Other times it seemed as if Stacie would block us from doing things, and I couldn't understand why. For example, although there was a swimming pool in their house, we were never allowed in there for some reason. Then one day Stacie went out to stock up on fuel, as there was a petrol strike about to start, and Dad said, 'Quick, boys, have a go in the pool if you like.'

We thought, 'Wow, this is amazing!' and were having the best time ever, leaping in and out, swimming around, just generally pissing about. I guess he thought Stacie would be gone for ages, stuck in a queue at the petrol station, but suddenly my dad was saying, 'Quick, boys, get out. Here's some towels, get upstairs and get dried off before Stacie sees ya.'

And we had to hide so that Stacie didn't know we had been

in the pool, because she didn't want us in there. I'm sure she had her reasons but as a kid I just felt as if she didn't want us to have fun. And I could never understand why Dad didn't put his foot down more. He is such an alpha male, you would expect him to always be the boss. The only way I can see it is that he fucked up his first marriage for Stacie, and he didn't want to ruin that relationship too, so he would do whatever it took to keep her happy.

It wasn't long after they had been in that house that Dad and Stacie got married and had a baby. I had to go to the wedding, but I can't say I liked it. It wasn't something I wanted to see. I knew Mum and Dad were never going to get back together, but to see Dad actually get a new wife, and one I didn't like . . . well, it was like it sealed everything. The woman who in my eyes had set out to destroy my family had finally succeeded. It was upsetting, especially for Mum. I remember her crying as I left to go to the wedding. If I'd had a choice I wouldn't have gone, but Dad wanted me there. Luckily he didn't push it and expect me to be a page boy or anything! It was just a straightforward registry office wedding and reception. The best bit about it was having a party with his side of the family.

Then on 5 April 2001 Stacie had their son, Mason, my half-brother, not that I can tell you much about him as a baby. Stacie was always saying, 'Don't let Kirk hold him. He'll drop him. I don't want Kirk near him.' At first I felt like I didn't know him. In fact, he is twelve now, and it is only in the last few years that I have been able to spend time with him and build a bond.

*

The longer we lived in the hostel, the stranger some of the people seemed to get, and the harder it all became. In the spring Mum got some kind of virus, and was in the toilet being really sick, and a woman just ran in and started hitting her. She was clinging on to the toilet seat, but this woman kept whacking her. I guess she was mentally disturbed, but it was weird. Not that I fully realized just how weird at the time.

After nearly a year, even Daniel and I were starting to get tired of the hostel and Mum was angry we hadn't been moved on. This dirty, often scary place wasn't supposed to be a permanent home, just somewhere for us to stay while the council found us a new house. But that hadn't happened.

Then one day my brother, who was fifteen by then, went across the road to Maxine's to borrow some orange squash for a school trip the next day. I was in our room upstairs when the buzzer went. I answered: 'Hello?'

'Kirk, open the door now!' I heard my brother gasp.

'What's up?'

'I've been shot.'

For some reason I broke into floods of tears and couldn't stop. Fear of what was about to come, I guess. We ran downstairs and he was out the front holding his chin, and the blood was pissing out, like really pulsing out of him, and he was pure white. Duncan and a mate of his, Phil, arrived at the same time, and someone said, 'Wayne shot him!'

We all sprinted to Wayne's room and Mum tried to kick the door open, yelling, 'You shot my son, Wayne! I will fucking kill you for this!'

We could hear him moving around inside, and just as Mum was kicking, the blade of a knife suddenly came through the door at her. He forced it right through the wood, trying to stab her. I couldn't believe what I was seeing and stood there rooted to the spot, completely terrified.

Phil pushed Mum out of the way and kicked the door in, and before Wayne had time to do anything, Phil picked him up and slammed him against the wall, screaming, 'You fucking little shitbag. What are you playing at?'

He kept picking him up and throwing him round the room like a rag doll, and I could see his head banging off the furniture. It only stopped when the police arrived to arrest Wayne.

Daniel was rushed to hospital and we finally found out exactly what had happened. It turned out army-obsessed Wayne had turned eighteen earlier that week and immediately went and got an air rifle. When Daniel was coming back to the hostel and saw him, he joked, 'Don't shoot me, Wayne!' But he did.

Daniel thought it was just a piece of cork that had hit him, but then he saw the blood. The bullet had gone through his chin and into his throat, a millimetre from his jugular. At the hospital they realized there was too much swelling to take the pellet out, so he had to lie in bed for four days to let the swelling go down, with this thing lodged in his neck, before they could operate. He was really brave about it but Mum was so upset.

In the meantime the police had released Wayne, saying he was mentally disturbed so they didn't want to jail him, and the hostel was the best place for him. Then Mum's crying stopped and she went mad. She stormed to the council and refused to leave.

'You want me and my sons to live in the same building as this mental idiot who shot my son! There is no security, only a few shit reception staff, and you think that is OK? You have to take us out before someone gets killed!'

She was so angry, I think she finally made her point. In the summer holidays a year after we had arrived, when I was twelve, we said goodbye to the hostel, and went on to the next stage of Essex life . . .

SIX

The Worst Estate in Essex

To get us out of the hostel, the council moved us to an estate called Seabrooke Rise, which I can't describe as anything other than a slum. If you live in Seabrooke Rise you are known to be scummy, it's as simple as that. Life there is like something out of the television show *Shameless* – this run-down council estate where everyone knows each other's business and all sorts of dodgy shit goes on.

If I was out of the area and told someone where I was from they wouldn't talk to me. They'd be scared to be associated with me, or of what I might do. But it didn't bother me. All my pals were from Seabrooke Rise anyway – all the people I had hung out with when we were in the hostel were from that area, and let's face it, no matter what people said about Seabrooke Rise, it was a step up for us.

The flats were arranged in rows of maisonettes. There were two flats on top of each other, with each family's flat made up of two floors. There were no road names – the whole area was just made up of different Seabrooke Rise blocks, then you got a flat number within that. The blocks were arranged in rows, and each row was a bit lower down the hill. There were about eight rows in total, with the tenants somehow seeming to get worse the further down the hill you got. The bottom row had all the real scuzzy ex-cons and druggies living in it. We were in flat 219, in the second row from the bottom.

And although the flats weren't the best accommodation in the world, as you can imagine, I thought they were pure luxury – because I got my own bedroom! Of course, being the youngest, I got the box room, but I didn't care. I had my own space for the first time in my life.

I was also happy to be physically further apart from Daniel. We hadn't been getting on for the last few years. We are very different people, and the three and a half year age gap was just a little too big to make it easy for us to be properly close when he saw me as the annoying little brother, while I saw him as the out-of-touch older brother. I'd even go so far as to say we hated each other at times, and our relationship could be really aggressive. We would fight every single day, and the older we got, the more physical the fights became. It would start off as a stupid argument over something as small as one of us being in the other's way, or sometimes even over nothing at all, then the abuse would get shouted louder and louder until one of us would take a swing at the other. And most of the time it would only stop when it had gone too far – I'd knocked Daniel out, or he had stabbed me in the arm with a chisel or butter knife, or whatever was to hand. If the fights had ever been filmed and shown on telly or YouTube, you would think it was so violent that one or both of us should be arrested. But that was just the way we got on with each other.

Mum would try to stop us, and would get angry and upset, but nothing got in our way once the two of us were rowing. We'd be totally focused on beating the other one, verbally or physically. It became a world with just two raging teenage lads in it, and we could only end it ourselves after we had followed it through.

As for our neighbours, they were mostly crackers. I soon learnt that the older kids who lived above us liked to spit. When I left the house I'd have to run quickly to the other side of the path, otherwise I'd end up with a minging load of flob on me. Another guy in the row of houses above us he used to sell fags to under-sixteens who couldn't get hold of them in the shops. L&Ms they were, as in Lambert & Butler, but we always used to say that stood for Lung Munchers really. I guess he got them on the cheap somewhere, and I would go round there for a packet, claiming they were 'fags for me mum' even though we both knew they weren't. They cost £1.20 a pack, which was good even in those days!

Just down from us was a bloke who used to sell drugs. By drugs I mean marijuana, not anything stronger. People always ask if there were loads of drugs where I grew up, which makes me laugh. The idea that poor areas are flooded with drugs is ridiculous – you need money for drugs, and when you can barely scrape together enough to pay for your weekly food, how on earth are you going to afford something expensive like cocaine?

As far as I was concerned cocaine was a faraway drug only taken by celebrities who drove around in Range Rovers – another thing I thought was confined to the realms of the rich and famous at that stage!

A lot of people had dogs, not all of them legal breeds, for a mix of reasons – protection, status or just plain good company.

But I was completely oblivious to the fact this wasn't how life was for kids all over Britain. I thought everyone apart from celebrities lived like this.

The area I grew up in, well, it was violent and poor. I always thought it was a good thing that Bella came back to live with us after we left the hostel. Although she was soft as shit, people are always a bit wary of a Staffie, so she was like extra protection for us.

For me, the worst thing when we first moved to Seabrooke Rise was the walk home from the train station after school. That is when people would be hanging around bored, looking for trouble. And while I did have friends there, I still wasn't a Seabrooke Rise local, and I would get into trouble. The area really was the ghetto of Essex. I would rather walk through the worst streets of London than walk through Grays.

On that walk home I would regularly get mugged or robbed. A gang of kids would appear out of nowhere, and I'd suddenly be surrounded.

'Take your shoes off.' One of them would get right up in my face, and snarl.

'Really?' I'd be so gutted at the idea of handing them over, but I was in no position to argue.

'Yes, I want those fucking trainers, so give them to me if you want to get past us!'

I'd have no choice but to take them off and walk home, head down, in my socks. The worst thing was getting in and seeing Mum's face, when she realized we were going to have to come up with the money for new shoes. We were still as badly off as ever. Mum was trying, though. She worked her arse off to make our lives better, and got a job as soon as we moved into Seabrooke Rise, working in community care. That meant she would go and look after old people in their own homes, helping them with their meals, or jobs they couldn't do themselves around the house, and just generally keeping them company and seeing they were all right. She was good at it, as she is such a caring person. And it was what she had trained to do before she met my dad and stopped work, so it meant she was finally getting back to her original ambition, which was great. But it was not amazingly paid, and we still struggled.

That was where the good side of the area came out, though. Despite the hellish environment, the absolute crap that we had to live through, people would still help each other. I don't want to make out that it was an amazing place and that everyone was one big happy family, but there was a sense that we were all in it together. It was like a lot of the old East End mentality from London, where everyone was poor but had each other's backs, had moved out to Essex at the same time as the old East Enders moved out that way. You would look out for your own and share what little you did have.

There were days when we would knock on the next door

neighbour's door and ask, 'You got a loaf of bread for me mum?' if we had run out, and Mum couldn't afford to do a shop.

Or someone might pop round to ours and ask Mum, 'You got a fiver I can borrow? The electric's gone and I've got nothing left this week.'

I know that sounds like the stereotype of a poor area turned good, but that was the reality of the situation.

I always liked the start of summer as well. Behind the houses where we lived there was a big communal garden, and each summer everyone would chip in and buy this big blow-up swimming pool from the local Costco, that all the kids would use. We all wanted to join together to make the sunny days that bit better for everyone. Then over the summer people just opened their homes to all the kids, so there was less of a divide and everyone kind of lived in all the houses, bouncing between them.

Poverty was all I knew, so I didn't question it or resent it. In fact I loved living there on some levels, and would never have changed it.

One of the best things about my life was my friends. I had a really good bunch of mates in Seabrooke Rise. There were about twenty of us who used to hang around together.

I don't trust a lot of people. I think I have been let down so often that I don't like to put too much faith in people doing the right thing or looking out for me. I know people can shit on you when it suits them, no matter how close you think you are. So it is better not to put them in a position where they can let you down in the first place. That's the way I have always thought about it, as it's what I learned growing up. So while my group of mates was great, our friendship was mostly about having a laugh together. There were just a few who were especially close, who I did trust, and who were more like brothers to me. They are the boys who are still in my life today.

My closest mate was called Ashton. He was the same Ashton I was friends with at primary school, and used to smoke with behind the green container, so when I moved to Seabrooke Rise I was really happy he was there too. I instantly knew I could rely on him, because we had history together.

Ashton was one of nine brothers and sisters, and they were all looked after by their mum, Sarah, who was a single parent, dealing with everything by herself. It must have been totally crazy for her, but she always seemed to cope and keep everything going in their family the way it should.

She was on benefits, and whenever my mum was complaining about her lot in life, going, 'I'm struggling bringing up you two, how am I going to cope on such little money? Life is awful!' and all that, I'd tell her, 'Just look at Sarah, you don't see her crying, and she has it a lot harder than you!'

One of Ashton's brothers, Reece, was a good pal of mine as well, and we used to hang around together. I knew those boys would have my back no matter what, and we would stand by each other. It also meant the muggings I had put up with when we first moved in only lasted for the first few months, until I became known as a local. I also quickly toughened up and learned to defend myself, so people didn't start on me a lot, but it was nice to know that if I needed them they would be there in a second to help out.

Sadly Reece passed away at a very young age. It is always so sad to see a good man go, and Reece really was a good man.

My other closest friends were also two brothers, called Zach and Kieron. My mum was friends with their mum, Charlotte, and it was a bit like they were our extended family.

Mum was still really down all the time because of the lack of money, so I would do anything I could to help her. I was only thirteen, so too young to get a part-time job at the weekends or anything, but I would try and think of other clever ways to get cash.

I never stole from shops or houses or anything, but I guess in a way – and this doesn't sound great – I did rob from my dad for her. She would suggest it sometimes when she was especially depressed, and short of cash for a bill or food.

She'd say, 'Kirk, we need money. Can you ring your dad up and get some somehow?'

I hated doing it, but my bad conscience over lying to my dad wasn't as bad as this sick feeling I had inside me, watching Mum constantly suffering because she had no money. Seeing her sink into more and more of a depression, and not being able to do anything, was horrible for a son. And again, that deep-rooted sense that I had to be the man of the house, and do whatever it took to make things better, would override anything else. So in the end I'd call Dad and think up an excuse, like, 'Dad, I've got a school trip tomorrow. Can I have some money for it?'

And he'd say, 'Well, not really, Kirk. I don't have a lot of cash going spare at the moment. Why do you need it?'

And I'd play on his softer side, and tell him, 'Oh please, mate, 'cos I look like a pikey if I ain't going on the trip, and everyone else is. Don't make me look like that, help me out!'

And he'd say, 'Oh, all right, then,' and he'd give me the money – and I'd give it straight to Mum.

I had conflicted feelings about doing this. I didn't want to lie to my dad, but in a way I liked the fact that I could do it, that I could help my mum out with something that she couldn't do herself. I was robbing to help my mum, and I'd still do it today if I had to. Besides, a bit of me felt like Dad had all this money, and I didn't understand why he wasn't helping her more. At one point he had loved her enough to marry her, and she was the woman looking after his kids.

As for me, I'd chop my arm off for my mum if it would help her. I would die for her, I reckon. She has been there for me through my whole life and I know she would do anything for me, and that is exactly what I feel for her too.

I had other ways of getting money, too, that didn't involve stealing off my dad. In fact, over the years my mates and I developed all sorts of ways to get extra cash. Not huge amounts, and not through out and out stealing. It was more a case of learning clever cons, ways to get hold of someone's money without mugging or robbing them. These are the things we needed to know to survive where we grew up.

One pretty basic technique we developed early on was getting the spare money from sweetshops. I'd go into one of the local newsagents that sold sweets, stand by the penny sweet counter – not that they exist these days, it is more like five pence a sweet! – and I'd drop a penny and let it roll under the counter. Then I'd make a big fuss about the fact I had dropped my money. 'Oh no! I've dropped all me money under the sweet stand! Mister, can you move it for us? It's the only money I brought with me, so it's the only way I can pay you!'

And sure enough the obliging shopkeeper would come and heave at the stand, pulling at it until he could shift it enough that we could get in underneath. And there would be my penny – along with plenty of other coins that people had dropped over the weeks since we had last tried this trick. Twenty-pence pieces, ten-pence pieces, and, if you were especially lucky, pound coins. And I'd scoop it all up as though it was all mine, rather than just the penny I had dropped under there, and walk out a few quid better off. It wasn't exactly proper theft – the person who had dropped it had chosen to leave it there, but that didn't make it the shopkeeper's either. Finders keepers!

Then we discovered phone boxes. At this time people were starting to get mobile phones, but not everyone was lucky enough to have one. So some people would still head to the phone box on the corner of their road to make their calls. We discovered that if you stuck something like a train ticket up inside the phone box it would stop the change coming out. Most people thought nothing of it if their twenty pence didn't appear – they just thought their call must have eaten into that money, so they wouldn't bother following it up. By the end of the day, in a popular phone box I could collect a couple of quid. Do that in a few phone boxes, and you are starting to look at not bad money for a teenager.

Then one of my mates and I escalated to using the same trick in a pub. His parents were the landlord and landlady of one that had an old flashing fruit machine in the corner. We decided it might work in a similar way to the phone box, so once when they weren't looking we got an empty fag box and shoved it up the slot where the money comes out. And, true enough, the first night we went back to check, we walked away with a result that made penny-sweet counters and phone boxes look like nothing.

It worked like this: when people won on the machine but didn't get their cash out, they would either think it was broken and accept that they had lost out on that money – rare, let's be honest – or they would go and complain, and my mate's parents would have to pay them the cash. No one ever thought to put their hand up inside the money shoot. But at the end of the day when the pub was shut and his parents weren't around, the two of us would sneak back in and pull the box out, and a shitload of money would come out.

It wasn't money that we had earned honestly, and of course I know that someone else was missing out for our benefit. But we were pretty creative and ingenious, I have to give my teenage self that. Besides, we didn't know what else to do. Our families

were all in the same boat, and that is pretty much what we had
to do to get cash.

There was fuck all for young people to do in the area, though
– especially for teenagers like us. The minute we were out of
school each day or on the weekend, we didn't have a clue what
to do with ourselves. We would hang around in the park, sit on
the swings and have a fag and just chat. It wasn't exactly exciting, but it beat sitting in the house staring at the television.

After a while the police started to come and have a go at
us. We had got quite big as a group, and the park was getting
taken over by gangs of kids hanging around with nothing else
to do. I can imagine it might have been a bit intimidating if a
mum did actually want to take her little kid in there, but we
were harmless really. Or my friends were, at least – we never
got into that much trouble at the time, but other lads in the park
did have fights, and we had even seen a few stabbings.

Someone would point to the other end of the park and
shout, 'Fuck, that fight looks like it's proper kicking off. That one
lad is proper getting it!'

Then a minute later, someone else would say, 'I think that's
a knife that guy on the left has got – shit, yeah, he just stabbed
that guy. Fuck, what if he killed him?'

And we'd all sit staring from our end of the park. We were
too fascinated to run away, but not brave enough to go over and
help. And in the end the police and the ambulance would turn
up and it would all be sorted.

Stabbings round there at that time weren't a rare thing.

Open the local *Gazette* every Friday and you would see a stabbing most weeks. I don't know if that was what made the police pay attention to us, or if we'd have been moved on anyway, but they started coming over as we were chilling out, and saying, 'There are too many of you hanging round in the park.'

'You know it's not us causing trouble?' we'd argue.

'These places are for kids, not teenagers.'

'Right, where would you like us to go? There are fuck all other places for young people to hang out.'

But the Old Bill would just shrug and make us move, and we would wander around, not sure where to go.

Sometimes we would head down to this boat yard near ours where some people kept their own boats. No fancy ones, and not owned by anyone in Seabrooke Rise, of course, but they made for a new place to hang out. There was a boathouse nearby where the posher boat owners would sometimes be, and they would go mad if they saw us. So we would sneak in when no one was looking and set up home in the boat of one unlucky owner for the evening.

We would raid the food cupboards, or if they were empty we'd put our own money together to get something, mainly bacon, and then cook food on the grill. Most of the boats would have a mini grill on board, and we quite fancied ourselves, sitting there making our meals. Other times we would set off the flares that were kept on board for emergencies, but that generally spelt the end of the evening, as it was a pretty obvious sign that we were there.

There was one wooden boat just over the wall from the boat

yard, on the bank of the Thames, that was a wreck. It had been there for years and we loved climbing over it. It was still pretty complete, and there was a crow's nest up at the top with ropes hanging down that we would swing right out on. I went back recently, though, and it has completely rotted away. No chance of finding the crow's nest on it now, let alone the ropes, sadly!

When we weren't climbing around some boat or other, we would set up camp in the stairs of the buildings around the estate and sit there having a smoke. After a while we moved on from smoking cigarettes to smoking pot. It was the fashion at the time, even if it was a bad one. We would all chip in a couple of quid, someone would be sent off to the flat of the guy who sold marijuana, and we'd go and smoke it.

I never had a lot of money to put into the mix, but sometimes I'd raid a pot that Mum kept for spare pennies. At the time I thought nothing of it, but now, knowing how little we had, I feel bad I took even those couple of quid I gathered together to put towards me smoking pot. But I never gave much thought to the bills that £2 could help with at that age. I just wanted to do my thing, and I thought I was fine to have some of that cash.

Luckily, though, marijuana was pretty cheap at the time. For £10 we could buy a block of hash – the guy sold it in solid form – and so add that to the fags and a packet of Rizlas, and we had an evening's entertainment for £11.40. Not that I would recommend that anyone spend their evenings smoking pot these days – it was just that it was the only thing on offer for us then.

SEVEN

A Teenage Boy's Dream

We spent two years in Seabrooke Rise, and all the time Mum was working hard, while Daniel and I were learning how to take care of ourselves. By the time I was fourteen, Mum was doing well in her job as a care worker, and was getting enough money that we were able to move out. Not far, mind – only a couple of streets away – but to a terraced house that wasn't completely paid for by the council like Seabrooke Rise had been. This time the council paid half the rent and Mum paid the other half.

It was called William Street, and we were at number 132. Don't imagine in any way that we were really moving up in the world, though. It was tiny – the width of the house was as small as the length of a car. And we soon realized the neighbours were an interesting sort – just a few doors down the house had been turned into a brothel!

So, being honest, this home was still a total dump. But it felt more like it was ours, and at least I could walk out the front door without being spat on from above. We even had a tiny back garden, although that was filled with tyres and mattresses, and whatever else people in the area dumped in all the gardens. But still, it was ours.

Daniel didn't move there with us. He was eighteen now, and really grown-up. He had been a bit of a wild boy in his own way as a teenager, getting on in the same way most of the lads around our way did, but then he seemed to decide he was going down the wrong path. So he put his nut down and got on with studying and then work. Daniel trained in welding, like my Dad, and was starting work for him at Delfini. He had a long-term girlfriend called Gemma, who was lovely, and he just suddenly seemed like an adult to me. Dad was really proud of him following in his footsteps, and was keen to do anything he could to help him, so he sorted him out with one of his flats in another part of Grays. It was one that he normally rented out, but instead he gave it to Daniel to live in.

I was not getting on well with Dad at all by this time, and really didn't see him that much. I was old enough that no one told me I *had* to visit him, so I chose not to go round to his place at weekends, and Dad didn't really push me to. I don't think either of us knew how to save a relationship that was getting worse and worse. I resented Dad, I still resented Stacie, and I was probably jealous of Daniel's relationship with him.

The move didn't change my day-to-day life in a big way. I was still hanging out with a group of mates in the stairwells, killing time. But even that started to change, because the police were trying to move us on from the staircases too, as if making the parks off limits hadn't left kids like us struggling to find somewhere to go. We tried to keep out of trouble, just doing our thing, but it seemed we weren't allowed to. We'd be sitting on the stairs and they would come and tell us we had to move on. That made us mad.

And I hold my hands up, that is when we did start being right little shits, just out of pure boredom. I'm not proud of it, and I know it is a cliché, but we really did have fuck all else to do, so we started running riot. I don't think we ever really thought about the consequences of everything we were getting up to – it was just something we did to pass the time then and there, which was stupid of us. So while I'd always had my ups and downs, it was now that I became a real pain in the arse, and not just for my mum, but society in general.

A few of us started standing by the roads, hiding behind bushes and stepping out at the last minute to throw stones at moving cars. I don't know what we got out of it, but somehow it was satisfying and funny at the time. We didn't actually want to cause an accident, and stupidly we didn't really think about the fact that it could be dangerous.

Then we moved on to smashing cars up, or breaking into them. We never tried to drive or steal them – we only broke into parked cars that we would then sit in, so that we had somewhere to be. Other times we'd rob motorbikes, even though we didn't know how to ride them, but we'd give it a go. It was just something to do. I know it wasn't great – I knew this even then, but I would ignore those feelings, as I simply didn't know how else to spend my time. And besides, everyone else was at it.

But worse than anything else was the fighting. Some of us

were always fighting. We didn't even care who with – most of the time it was just a stranger who walked past at the wrong time, but afterwards the poor guy would wish he hadn't. We were nightmare kids. If you were a decent person with a job, who had to walk through our area to get to work, you'd have hated us. We were the little shits who sat on the wall, spitting. The idiot teens who would get up as you walked past and crowd around you, pushing you and giving you hassle for no reason, doing anything to intimidate you. Or other times we would get into proper fights, with other groups of boys from round the area. I admit I even got a release out of it. The pent-up anger and aggression that would flare up in me as a kid was still there. Put me on a street in these situations, and, well, it is too easy to just let it out.

And even though I know why I did it in a way – as well as my anger, we were young, bored and trying to assert ourselves as men – that is no excuse. I am ashamed about what we did – and that a poor person on their way to work couldn't just get there without us kicking off and ruining their day.

This is one of the reasons why now I would love to work with kids from estates like Seabrooke Rise. I understand what they are thinking and going through, and why they get angry and violent. I would like to go and talk to them, and find out what their hopes and dreams and talents are, and see if there is something that can be done to use their skills and make things happen for them.

People do always have another part of them that needs to be drawn out – no one is a completely violent little yob. Despite the way I was out in the street, I had a very different side. I would still go round to my nan's and bake cakes. I was obsessed with it! I loved making them with her while chatting away about life. It was kind of therapeutic.

I also did one other thing that was completely at odds with the version of me that my friends saw. I collected cat ornaments. How weird does that sound? I was obsessed with cats, and I'd save my money to collect these cats and line them all up on my shelf in my bedroom. I loved my collection!

So there I would be, fighting in the street, then coming in and cleaning my ornaments. Shouting abuse at people in the street, then heading to my nan's to bake a cake. There is a reason I have always said I am like Jekyll and Hyde with my double personality, and it was showing as much as ever at that age!

It would still come out at home as well, which is the one thing that I hated. I didn't like my mum seeing me when the anger would take over and I would lose it. I could be fine one minute, and the next I would go mad. It makes me really ashamed. But I wouldn't go for Mum in our rows – I would take it out on our house instead. The doors in William Street especially took a beating from me. Battering them was the only thing that would stop me in my rampage. Once I ripped a door off its hinges. Can you believe I did that? It must have been quite a scary sight to see this crazed teen tear a door away from the wall. There were no doors left in the house after we had been there for a few months, not even a bedroom door. Even the front door, which was the only one still in place, didn't work properly.

Once when I was going mad Mum had locked me out, tired of dealing with me. She'd given up trying to talk to me, and thought if she left me outside for a bit I would calm down and realize I needed to behave better. But what did I do? Boot the door off its hinges! It was like I got super-human strength in my rage. My mind was filled with anger, and nothing else. So that was that door bust. Every night we had to screw it locked.

My poor mum's house was fucked. She was struggling to keep it nice and all I was doing was following in this crazy trail behind her and demolishing the place. I was horrible to her when she was trying her hardest. That she stuck by me and kept on dealing with it is one of the amazing things about her.

I did have one friend who was a really positive influence and who, as I got to know him, gave me a new focus in life, which meant I wasn't only hanging about in the street. Around this time I started becoming good friends with an old mate of my brother's called Ashley Brown. He was four years older than me, and I had looked up to him for a few years. When he had been friends with Daniel, back when we lived in Seabrooke Rise, my brother had not let me near him. Daniel was a wannabe DJ at the time – he had a set of decks in his room that Dad had bought him, and he was always practising on them. Ashley was an MC called Skolla B, who was really famous around our area. Even if you had never met him, you knew about him. Everyone rated him and he did all the parties, MC'd at local pubs, the under-eighteens parties, everything. Drum and bass music was all the craze at the time, and I mean proper craze. Kind of like Justin Bieber is to people today! Everyone wanted to be an MC, but Ashley was at the top of the tree in our area. The rest of us had to make do with MP3 players with little speakers attached, which we would tuck inside our hoods and walk down the street with it turned right up and the music blasting out. *Wudda wudda wudda! Budda budda budda!*

I'm sure we looked like thugs, but every generation has someone like that – before us it was people with their boom boxes and cassette tapes – which I had always thought was cool when I was a little kid!

So we were obsessed with Ashley, as he was our main source of inspiration for that music. But no matter how many times he was round our house, there was no way Daniel was letting me in his room, so I never got to hang out with him. To him I was just Daniel's little brother. So I had to sit in the next room, my bedroom, a proper fan, but not allowed to speak to him.

Once Daniel had left home and I was living in William Street, though, I got to be good friends with Ashley, finally! And he would come round after school, and then it was me with my decks, messing around with him. Dad had got me a set of decks too by then – as we got older he became more generous with money, although there was still no moving him when it came to my mum. Mum and I still had no money, but life seemed a bit easier when he would buy me things like that to have at home. It gave me encouragement, and made me feel like our money situation wasn't so bad after all.

And I think the whole MC'ing scene was great for me. It gave me something to do after school other than just hang around, have fights and cause trouble. And it was good as well because my mum loves Ashley – they get on really well. She even calls him her third son and he calls her 'Mum', and she gave him the spare key to our front door. After that, a lot of the time I would get home from school and he'd be in the house already. He's definitely my best pal, even today, and although he is four years older I've never noticed. If I'm upset he is the first person I'd call.

I started going out to parties with Ashley, which I loved. Mum was always very chilled about me going places, getting the train around, staying late, coming home when I wanted, that kind of thing. She knew I could look out for myself – and that really there was no point her trying to stop me anyway. If I wanted to go out, I would!

I was nearly fifteen years old, and had reached the age where I was desperate to have sex. All the boys were apparently at it, and everyone but me seemed to have slept with someone. Looking back I'm sure most of them were making it up – I think I even claimed I had slept with someone too, even though I hadn't, just to make myself sound hard. But the reality was, secretly I was desperate for it to happen so I could say it for real to my mates with my head held high, and so that I would know for myself what it was really like. The problem was – who with?

Then the week before Valentine's Day 2003 everyone kept talking about this girl called Sarah. One mate told me, 'She is a right little goer. She has already slept with a couple of people!'

'Two people already? No way!'

'Yup,' he told me. 'Go out with her and there's a good chance you are going to get sex.'

Well, the idea kept playing on my mind. It was hardly likely to be the romantic first-time sex you see in the movies, but at least it would have happened. And I figured with Valentine's Day coming up, now might be as good a time as any . . . So when I bumped into her on Friday 14 February I plucked up the courage and said to her, 'Will you start seeing me?' Because that was the way you said it then.

'Yeah, all right.' She shrugged, as though she wasn't bothered, but would do me the favour.

Result! 'Yeah, I am seeing her!' I thought. 'I am on my way to having sex for the first time . . .'

Then I thought I'd move it up a level. 'You might as well be my girlfriend if you're seeing me, then,' I casually said to her.

'Yeah, all right.' She shrugged again, as though this was also pretty unimportant to her.

Well, it was pretty damn important in my mind. That night we did our usual and went out in East Tilbury. At the time that's what we all did. It was annoying for me as it was two train journeys away from where I lived, but if I wanted to hang out with everyone, I had to do it. I wasn't the only one from my area who went, though – most of my Seabrooke Rise gang headed there too. So we would all get on the train together, and of course we didn't have the money to pay for it, so we were bunking. But by that time we were such an imposing lot, ten scally kids getting on the train in a group, none of us paying, that the ticket inspector would ignore us, assuming that we were just little thugs who should be left alone.

Then in East Tilbury we would always go to the park – the police over that way weren't so strict – and I met up with Sarah that night in our group. Hardly the most romantic Valentine's date, but there you go, I knew no different. And we stayed there for a while, just drinking the usual weekend park drinks – big bottles of White Lightning or 20/20 – until I said to her, 'Do you want to go for a walk?'

'Yeah, all right,' she shrugged. I was beginning to think they were the only words she knew. But she wasn't stupid – we both knew what was going to happen when we headed off on our walk together, awkwardly hand in hand.

And fucking hell, the next bit is so unromantic, and to be honest, as grim as you like, that I'm embarrassed to tell it. But I have promised to be honest in this book, so here goes . . .

All I knew about sex was what I had learnt from mates and through school and movies, so although I had a rough idea, I can't exactly say I knew what I was doing. But I took her behind this green container in the park – yep, another green container! Like I said, they were everywhere, and seemed to play a huge part in my young life . . . Now when people asked, 'Where did you smoke?' 'Behind the green container,' 'Where did that fight happen?' 'Behind the green container,' and all that, I could add, 'Where did you first have sex?' 'Behind the green container,' to that list!

So behind this container was a load of rubbish that people had dumped over time, including a table with only two legs at

Above Mum and Dad, looking happy together.

Left Getting a cuddle from Dad.

Below That's me in the back garden of our house in Jesmond Road, about to get into Oscar's kennel!

Left With my big brother Daniel on the way to a fancy dress party. Guess who I'm meant to be? Bart Simpson, obviously!

Below In the pool with Dad's mum, Nanny Pernod.

Below I was proud of my school uniform, as you can see from this photo taken on my first day at school.

Below right With our lurcher, Oscar, and Daniel.

Left In the kitchen with Nan and Granddad, Mum's parents.

Below With Daniel: the men of the house now Dad had left.

Bottom My sixteenth birthday, with a cake and a big hug from Mum.

Right Aged sixteen – note the hair gel. Spikes were big in Essex that year.

Below Dressed up for the school prom – I looked like Dr Evil from the *Austin Powers* films!

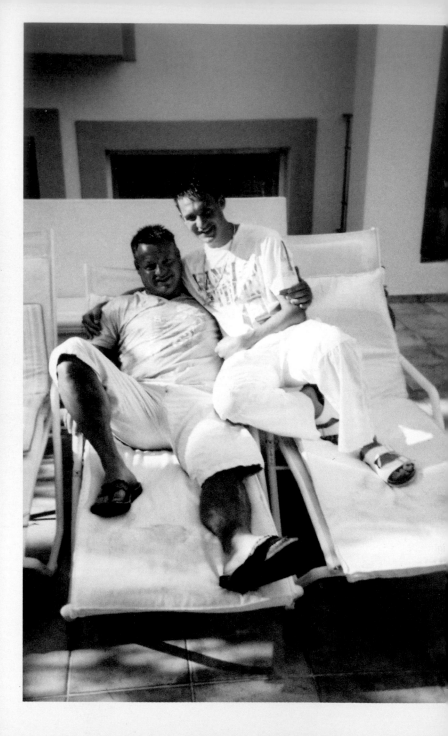

ft With Dad in Ibiza – our
st proper holiday together
and I loved it. He was
becoming my best mate.

Above At Sugar Hut with
iam McGough, twins Sam
d Amanda Marchant and
rian Belo, who were all in
Big Brother series eight.

ight Chantelle Houghton
as been known to come
Sugar Hut too! An Essex
irl who has made a great
career for herself.

Above Some of the cast at the launch of *The Only Way is Essex* in autumn 2010. From the left: Sam Faiers, Lauren Goodger, Jessica Wright, me, Mark Wright, Candy Jacobs and Amy Childs.

Below With Dad, who joined *TOWIE* in 2011.

bove With Lauren Pope. When I first
et eyes on her, I just thought 'wow'.

Above right With Lauren again, at
Sugar Hut in May 2011. It was the
wrap party for the end of the
spring series of *TOWIE*.

ar right Lauren and I
th booked in to have
se jobs – I'm looking
retty out of it here.
here was a lot more
ain afterwards than
I'd imagined.

ight My Bettie Page
tattoo, which I had
made to look a bit
like Amy Childs as
a tribute to her!

Right Leaving Sugar Hut alongside Amy in August 2011. She'd left *TOWIE* and was about to go into the *Celebrity Big Brother* house. We became mates again after that.

Below With Joey Essex who felt like my little brother when he first joined *TOWIE*.

Top right On a date with Gemma Massey at the Winter Wonderland in Hyde Park on 28 November 2011. I couldn't get her out of my head.

Far right Holding hands with Natasha Giggs after the *Celebrity Big Brother* wrap party on 16 February 2012. She's a really nice girl.

Right Sam and Billie Faier, two great girls and good mates!

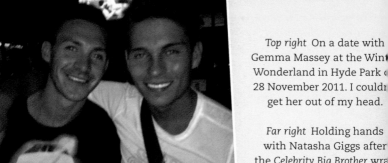

Above Dappy always supports me and I try to do the same for him.

Below Danny Dyer has become like an older brother to me.

one end, so it was slanted like a slide. I lay on it on my back and half took my trousers down. When you were a kid you didn't want to get naked, so I didn't even have them below my knees.

Then we fumbled around, I think I got it right, then a couple of seconds later it was done. No protection, no romance, no foreplay, but I was no longer a virgin. It wasn't my best performance, but it didn't matter. I had had sex. And that was it – I walked back to my mates, strutting like a criminal who had just killed someone and was proud of it. I had this swagger and was as cocky as you like for the rest of the night – like a 'Come on, boys, you want to feel my biceps?' kind of attitude. It is so embarrassing looking back. If any of my mates got on like that now, I'd rip them for it. But I knew no better.

By the end of the evening I had dumped her. That sounds so bad, doesn't it? It was awful to be that shallow, but I had only gone with her to lose my virginity. Not that I think she cared anyhow. This is how the conversation went:

Me: 'Sorry, Sarah, I don't think you're right for me. I'm breaking up with you.'

Her: 'Yeah, all right.'

And that was it.

Then after that night, it was like the floodgates opened and I couldn't stop having sex. I became a bit obsessed with it, and with women in general, like some kind of teenage nymphomaniac. But the grimness of the sex didn't improve after my first experience. I was sleeping with any girl I could, anywhere possible – in bushes, in elevators, in empty flats, in the bin sheds

. . . Anywhere and everywhere that you could have sex, I did. But romance and love? That never came into it. It's not like I was being rude, or a player, taking advantage of all the girls, because they were just as bad. Everyone was sleeping with everyone. It was like we hit fifteen and life became a massive seedy orgy in Grays.

I think it was because it gave people a new thing to do. A way to pass the time.

At that age, I knew everyone in the area. Even if I wasn't mates with a girl, I knew her. And I would try my luck with them all. I'd be on my own just getting a burger in the town centre and I'd see a bird I'd met once before and I'd say something cheeky like, 'You wanna come and sit on those stairs and wank me off?'

And more often than not the girl would be bored, and just go, 'Yeah, all right.'

But that was just Grays back then. Dirty, grim, but like a bored and frustrated teenage boy's dream.

I especially loved having sex, because – and I'm not boasting – I was pretty advanced in the downstairs department. My penis then was like a man's penis. It was ridiculous but I loved it and I wanted everyone to know it. I wanted to show as many girls as I could, and after sex, when they complimented me on my size, I would say, 'You tell your mates about me. You fucking tell 'em, love!' It gave me a massive confidence boost to know I had that kind of advantage over other lads.

And I was clocking up the numbers. I have no idea how

many girls I have slept with since the day I lost my virginity, but it has never really stopped, apart from the odd serious relationship along the way. If I had to guess I'd say I have slept with 800 to 1,000 girls. That sounds like a lot, but I love sex so I don't regret it. And when I am in a relationship I behave myself, and I think that is what is important. Enjoy yourself when you are single, but when you are with one person, make sure you are true to them.

But the thing was, not one of these girls meant anything to me – and I didn't mean anything to them. I wasn't too bothered about that, until I came across the first girl who ever really blew me away when I was fifteen years old . . .

Ashley had to MC at a party in Stanford-le-Hope and he asked if I wanted to go with him. Well, I did, as usual, because I loved going along to nights like that with him, and soon after we arrived I spotted these three quite exotic-looking brunette girls. Even though they were triplets, it was one of them more than the others that I noticed. Two of them were practically identical, but the third, while she looked like them, was even more stunning, a bit different there was something about her. She had amazing long brown hair and brown eyes, and looked gorgeous.

'Ash, I need to meet that girl, bloody hell, my God, she is . . .' I stopped, lost for words. 'I actually think I have fallen in love with her.'

And I swear, that's what it was like. I had never got that feeling from looking at a girl before. Ashley laughed at me, but he sorted it out that we were introduced. It turned out she was called Aisha, and although she lived in the area, her family were originally Turkish. We got on straight away, and she was really bubbly and fun and had a cute laugh. Luckily it seemed like she fancied me, and before I knew it, I had ignored my nerves and plucked up the courage to ask her out, and she was my first proper girlfriend.

There was no such thing as going on proper dates back then in Grays. It just wasn't the thing to do. Kids in Grays don't do dates – they are for adults, or posh people. Besides, we weren't old enough to get in anywhere decent, and no one had the money to go to a nice restaurant or the theatre or whatever anyway, even if they wanted to. For us, being boyfriend and girlfriend meant walking round town holding hands, stopping in the bus stop to kiss. Most days I would go home after school and get ready, doing my hair as best as I could to look half decent. Then I'd get on the train on my own and hang out with Aisha for the evening.

I really did develop strong feelings for her, and I suppose I did love her, although looking back it was still very much a teenage romance. It was the first time I ever thought about a girl when I wasn't with her, and felt emotionally connected to her. I also stopped messing around with other girls, as I didn't want to hurt Aisha, and anyway I wasn't interested. As far as I was concerned, I had the best already. I did sometimes think, 'Oh my gosh, this must mean I am becoming an adult!'

It wasn't all plain sailing – we did have the odd row, and we split up a few times – but mostly, especially during the school holidays when we had lots of time to spend together, we were pretty full on.

So all in all life was good, mostly filled with my girlfriend and MC'ing.

EIGHT

Finding My Way in the World

There was never any question that I was going to leave school as soon as humanly possible. I was counting the days to get out into the real world almost from the first week I started there. I'd been kicked out of pretty much every class going, as I didn't enjoy any of them, and I was useless at them all, so made up for it by being naughty. The only thing I liked was art, even though I wasn't very good at it. In fact for the last couple of years of school, because I had been thrown out of so many other classes, half the time they just sent me to the art rooms and said, 'You might as well just go and spend your time in there, because it's the only place you aren't naughty. To be honest, do what you like, because we're sick of you.'

I liked the feeling of independence I had when I was doing art. I could work on my own and at my own pace, and it wasn't a straightforward matter of getting it right or wrong, so I didn't feel like I was being judged, like I did in the other classes. I could express myself a bit through it too, and I didn't feel like I had a teacher breathing down my neck the whole time. But I didn't want to go on and study it further. Art was just the best of a bad bunch to me. I wanted to be out in the real world, living and working like my dad did. I had to sit my GCSEs first, though. I knew I wasn't going to get decent grades in any of them and it was a waste of time even attempting. I just thought the quicker I got through the exam paper each time, the better.

We also had the school prom once the exams were out of the way, to mark the end of our school life. Everyone else dressed up in proper black suit, white shirt and black bow-tie combos, but my mate and I decided to be different. He went all in white, and I found a grey suit that I thought looked smart at the time. I have only realized since it was pretty much an exact copy of the one worn by Dr Evil in the *Austin Powers* films . . . The party itself was a good laugh, though.

Of course I didn't just go to the prom, I went on to another party afterwards, and was out all night – which was not rare for me by then. The after-party doesn't stick in my mind, but I do remember exactly what happened when I got home at dawn. As usual Bella was there to greet me, but she didn't seem the same and was just hanging her head. When I looked closer she was covered in weird lumps, all over her skin. It was like some kind of insect had attacked her in the night. I called Mum, and she came down all sleepy, and then woke up with shock when she saw the state of Bella.

'You're right, she doesn't look good at all, poor thing! I'll get her off to the vet right now.'

Mum got dressed, put Bella on a lead and headed off. I felt

on edge after she had gone, because I could tell whatever was wrong with Bella was serious. A few hours later I heard Mum come back in, and went to see her, but she was standing there alone, with just the lead in her hand.

'I'm sorry, Kirk,' she said. 'Poor Bella was filled with cancer. Apparently those lumps were cancer all over her skin. The vet said the only thing to do was put her down.'

Well, I'm not lying, I cried like a baby. I loved that dog to bits and was totally gutted to lose her. She was fourteen and had lived a good life, but she had been present in mine as far back as I could remember, so to lose her was like losing a member of my family. It might sound ridiculous, but I felt like I had lost my sister. I went into proper mourning for her.

Eventually I decided the best way to get over her was to convince Mum we needed a new dog – if we replaced Bella, it might make losing her that bit easier. Besides, as it was just the two of us in the house by then it was a bit lonely. I figured we needed a third living creature in with us, and I love dogs. So we went down to the RSPCA and took a look at their rescue dogs. I don't see the point in buying one off a breeder if you can get an abandoned dog that needs a home.

We fell in love straight away with a dog there called Storm, a Labrador–Staffie cross. She had been abandoned and they said she was well behaved, so we took her home. Well behaved, my arse! She was a proper little terror from the minute we walked into the house. She was always biting and tearing things to bits. One of the first things she went for was Oscar, the little stuffed dog Nanny Pernod had bought me when I was only a few years old. I went mad. That toy had been with me most of my life, and I don't mind admitting that I'd still sleep with him when I wanted comfort, even by that age. If I was ill, or had been out and had a fight, I'd say, 'Mum, where's Oscar? I need him today.' And I wouldn't stop moaning until she found him for me. It didn't exactly go with my streetwise image, but as I've said, there are two sides to me.

Storm then went for my trainers as well – they were a new pair that Mum had been saving to buy for ages, and she totally shredded them. We couldn't see any way to train her. This dog just wanted to sit and destroy things! But it wasn't only belongings she kept biting – she went for people too. And I don't mean little nips, I mean tearing-people-to-bits type bites. So after she had attacked the postman and a neighbour, we decided we couldn't handle her and took her back. We clearly weren't going to be able to replace Bella as easily as I had thought. So instead we got ourselves two cats and they were much more of a success. Finally I had real cats, rather than just the models that filled my room!

After this, the six-week school holiday started. It wasn't really a holiday for me, as I wouldn't have to go back to school at the end of it, but I certainly started off treating it like one! I was spending time with Aisha, hanging out with my mates and doing everything but think about my future and my career. I had no idea what I wanted to do or be in my life, so I was trying to ignore the whole question.

Instead, I wanted to start with some other changes that I

thought might make me more of an independent, grown-up man. One of the first was to come off Ritalin. I had been on it for five years by then, and felt I had given it enough of a go. I still knew it only delayed my anger, and I thought I would rather just be myself. Also the idea that it was impressive to be on it, that it made me hard and tough to take these pills each day, seemed daft as I got older. Now it made me feel a bit of a kid, having to take these stupid pills every day because I couldn't control myself.

So I told Mum I was going to come off it, but I didn't discuss it with the doctors or anything – I just stopped taking it. I noticed a difference, of course I did, but mostly in a good way. I felt like I was going back to the real me, and I've never touched it since.

But the no job, no college thing wasn't washing with Mum. She gave me a few weeks' cooling-off period after school, then she was on my case. She was keen that I should carry on study-ing, as she knew there was very little chance of me getting a job without at least some qualifications, so each day she would say to me, 'You need to enrol in college. What are you going to do?'

I'd always shrug, and say, 'I ain't got a clue. There's nothing I want to do.'

And it was true. There was nothing that had ever really inspired me. I had no great dreams to do any particular job at all. I liked the idea of doing something where I was pretty inde-pendent, maybe a businessman like my dad, but that was it. I wasn't getting on that great with him at the time, but I thought he might have an idea, so I rang him one day and said, 'Dad, help me out here, please. What the fuck am I going to do now school is over?'

And I should have guessed his answer before I even called. Sure enough he said, 'Do what your brother is doing – do welding.'

'Dad, I don't want to do that, it's not my kind of thing.'

Despite all the fighting and everything, I've never been a real man's man – I've always been a bit of a pretty boy when it comes to getting my hands dirty. But in the back of my mind I started thinking, 'Maybe I should do that after all, because Dad loves Daniel for going down the family business route.' The whole of Dad's family thought Daniel was the golden boy, which I did resent deep down a bit, I guess.

So I was playing around with the idea, swinging each day between thinking it was a good idea or bad one, until one day I was sitting at home, just flicking through the newspaper, and Mum came in and said, 'Right, you have to enrol in something today, once and for all. What's it going to be?'

I tried to ignore her, and carried on going through the paper. I was so pissed off with the whole conversation, I just kept hoping someone would come up with a magic answer.

And then something caught my eye. It was a picture of boxer Lennox Lewis fighting a Russian opponent, Vitali Klitschko. Lewis had won, after badly cutting Klitschko's face with a punch, and the photographer had caught the exact moment of impact, and the shock in Klitschko's eyes. I was fascinated by it, and felt the photographer had done the perfect job.

'Mum,' I said, 'I want to be a sports photographer.'

'Don't just say that to come out with an answer and shut me up, 'cos it won't work, Kirk!'

But I felt sure, and said, 'No, if I could ever capture a picture like that, that would be my aim, that's what I want to do.'

She looked at the paper, then grinned, patted me on the shoulder and said, 'Right, well, you have a goal now – good. Let's go tell the college!'

So we went over to Thurrock Technical College to ask how I could get on a photography course. There were already long queues of students, so I clearly wasn't the only person making a late decision! This woman behind the desk told me, 'You need two C grades in your GCSE results to get on the photography course, and one of those must be in art, and one in science.'

I was thinking, 'Fuck me, I know I won't get that.' But our results weren't due for a good few weeks, so I said, 'Yeah, I'll have that fine, no problem.'

She got me to fill out some forms and enrolled me, and as I was leaving she said, 'Of course, we'll need proof of your results. So you can start the course, but once the certificates come through, you'll need to bring them in and show us if you are to continue.'

So the course started. Most of my mates from school were in the college too, all on different courses, and I was actually looking forward to starting mine in a way. If it could teach me how to do a job I wanted to do, that was all good. I'd looked at more photos since that boxing one, and seen a few sports shots that I really liked. For the first time in my life there was a career I could see myself doing: a sports photographer.

But on the first day at college, as I sat down in the class and waited for them to hand out the cameras, the teacher started to explain how to use all these photography programmes on the computer, and how Macs worked. I didn't have one at home, and I wasn't about to be able to afford one either.

I sat through this for a few days, but as it went on and on, I started to get frustrated. I said to the teacher, 'I don't mean to be rude, but I don't get the point in teaching me this when I want to be a photographer, not work with computers. Teach me how to use a camera properly, please, 'cos I can't afford a computer, so I can't use all this stuff you're showing me.'

'No, using the camera comes later in the course,' he replied. 'First we learn the computer side of things, then it will be about various lenses. And finally once you have all the basic info, we let you have a go with a camera.'

Well, as usual, I said what I thought. 'I don't care about all that. Give me a camera in my hand and let me see if I can take decent pictures, 'cos if I can't, there's no point in me doing the course if I only find out in a few months that I can't even take a good picture and I'm wasting my time!'

Naturally they weren't going to change the course because of some idea that I had about how it should be. So – and as you will know, this is rare for me – I decided to bite my tongue and go with it for the time being.

Then suddenly, I had something much bigger to deal with.

I hadn't seen Aisha during the first week of college, but I

hadn't expected to, as her whole family had gone on holiday to Turkey for a few weeks at the end of the summer. Then, in the second week, a mutual friend came running up to me in the corridor.

'Have you heard about Aisha?' he asked.

'No, what?'

'She's had a car crash in Turkey. She's dead. Her sisters are alive, but in hospital, proper badly injured. I'm sorry, mate.'

I stared at him, unable to take it in. Then my brain just crumbled and I had to get out of college. I ran out, crying as I went. I was so devastated. I went straight home and proper cried like a baby for the rest of the day. It was such a raw feeling of pain, I didn't know what to do with myself. I kept thinking how unfair it was on this lovely beautiful girl that she should die so young. I was in a bad way and Mum was away on holiday at the time so I was on my own. But Ashley was great – he was there for me, and came round all the time to check on me and try to cheer me up over the next couple of weeks. It was a long time before I stopped thinking of Aisha and missing her.

Meanwhile, my course teacher was on my case for proof of my two GCSE grades, but I just kept saying I didn't have the certificates from my school yet. Of course I did, and I knew I hadn't got what I needed. My results had been a whole load of Ds, Es and fails, as I had expected. So I don't know how I thought I'd get away with lying, but I just kept putting off telling them, until one day they asked again, and I said, 'I called this morning to chase up, but they still haven't passed them on, so I ain't got them.'

'Is that right, Kirk?' the teacher asked. 'Or do you know you don't have the right grades, so you're not telling me, as you'll have to leave the course? Because I actually called your school this morning. And they told me you do have your results.'

Well, there was no point lying after that!

'OK, yeah, I lied to you. I just don't see why I need those subjects, they have nothing to do with photography. It makes sense if I want to do science that I need science or whatever, but not for this course.'

I'd tried, but he just stayed silent and looked at me. 'OK,' I sighed, knowing I had lost this one. 'What do I do now?'

'You have to do an art foundation course for a year and get a C or higher, and then you can come back on this course.'

Well, that was it – I exploded, and the mouthy prick side of me came out. 'No way, for two reasons. I'll be a year behind all my mates, with younger kids in my class, and I'll look like I'm a stupid kid held back a year. And two, I'm shit at art, as you can see from my GCSE result. I can't draw, so why am I going to do any better at it this time round? I'll just fail it again!'

The problem with art for me was that on one level I loved it. I do have a really creative mind, and that's why I was happy to do it at school. Give me spray cans and a big canvas, as they did, and I can make brilliant pictures, but give me a pencil and tell me to draw, and it's a nightmare. I had an image of this art course at college, all these proper artists sitting round doing pencil drawings of naked male models. Not what I was up for!

135

We had a bit of a barney about it, but in the end I knew I had to do it if I wanted to be a photographer. So finally I said, 'Oh, for fuck's sake, give me the art course, and I'll do it.'

So I swapped on to the art course. I was a week or two behind the others, but the idea was that I should be able to catch up. In the first lesson I asked to have a word with the teacher, as I thought it was best to be straight up about the situation – I was shitting myself about the course, as everyone else on there really liked art, and was actually good at it. So I said to him, 'Look, I'm only doing this course so I can do photography. I can't draw.'

'I understand, don't worry,' he assured me.

'And the other thing is, I'm embarrassed how bad I actually am, so if you don't hold my work up to other people or anything, I'd appreciate it.'

And he nodded and agreed.

Then the lesson started, and we had to sit around this bowl of fruit and draw it. I was thinking, 'Are you having a fucking laugh? I can't even draw one piece of fruit, let alone a whole bowl.' But he told me to 'just draw what you see in front of you', so I decided to give it a go. And I drew something that to be honest I can't even describe. It looked like nothing I know, certainly not a fruit bowl, anyway! I was trying to do the bowl, but I'll be fucked if I could see a fruit bowl appearing on my piece of paper. I could probably have done it better with my eyes shut. And the more I tried, the worse it was getting, until eventually I got so frustrated, I called the teacher over.

'Look, sir, my drawing is shit! There's no way I can do this for a year and walk away with a C. What am I supposed to do to make it better?'

And he picked it up and studied it, then said loudly, 'Right, ladies and gentlemen, if I could have everyone's attention. If you could all look at Kirk's drawing, we have an example here of what not to do.'

Oh my God, I lost my fucking temper! Though I can't blame myself, when he was about to do what I had especially asked him not to. I grabbed my drawing back, screwed it up and threw it across the class. Then I turned to him, and said, 'See you, you're a prick.'

And that was it – I walked out. I was so angry. I felt humiliated and upset, and as always, rather than cry, I had let my frustration come out in a different way. I thought, 'I need out of college. There's no way I am going to survive two years of this place,' and I started walking towards the exit. I decided to call Dad on my mobile to tell him, 'Listen, I've fucked it, and I don't know what to do now. Any ideas?' But just as it was ringing through at his end, I walked past the welding course, and I saw my mate Olly in there, who I had grown up with, and made a decision on the spot. 'Yes! My mate is on that course, that will be way more fun. And if I tell Dad I'm finally swapping to that, doing what he told me to do in the beginning, he'll be well happy.'

So I called, and Dad answered from Heathrow Airport. He was about to get on a plane to fly out to America to watch the 2004 Ryder Cup in Detroit, so he couldn't talk for long, but I had time to say, 'Dad, just to let you know, I've sacked off art, and I'm gonna do a welding course for ya, and I will come and work for you after if that is OK.'

And he said, 'Fucking hell, boy, go on! You get in there and enrol for it, and I'll give you a job one day a week at my yard while you're doing the course as well. Be good experience.'

And I could hear in his voice that he was really proud of me, so I knew I had made the right choice. Both his sons were going to have done welding and be part of the family business. This was his dream!

'And you know what,' he continued, 'I'm going to bring you back a present from the US. You know iPods aren't out in the UK yet? Well, they are over there, so I'll get you one as a well done.'

I hung up from that call really happy with my decisions – and the idea of the iPod! – and went straight off to re-register myself for my third course of the term: welding. And, well, I got stuck into that and liked it – at first.

I was quite enjoying college for the social side of things. There was a whole group of us that were really into the same music scene, and we would have rap battles on our breaks in between the obligatory lunch from the local chippy that everyone had, pretty much every single day – chips, cheese and gravy. I loved that! I wore tracksuits below my arse, and talked like I thought I was a stereotype of a black rapper. I'd kiss my teeth, spit on the floor and go, 'What's happenin', blud? You sweet?' I was that kid your parents didn't want you to be friends with, and my mum would mock me, walking past and pretending not to see me, and then going, 'Oh, sorry, Kirk, I didn't recognize you there for a minute.'

But I didn't care. I thought I was a rapper, and all my crew were at the same thing. My name was MC Fait, which Ashley chose for me. I liked that name.

I was also taking my interest in MC'ing to a new level, and had started working on a pirate radio station, which was brilliant. Pirate radio was massive at the time, and despite being illegal I think it is really good for young people. It gives you a chance to do something that makes you feel important – something that feels like an actual career, and that you care about – and it's a place to hang out without getting into trouble.

Pirate radio stations can be set up anywhere. The typical ones in London are in a tower block in someone's flat, or in a deserted warehouse in the middle of nowhere. But the one I was on, called Renegade FM, was in a room in an old building in the middle of a farmer's field.

I'd go down there whenever I could, and talk on the radio and MC. Ashley and I started having a regular slot between 8 p.m. and 9 p.m., one evening a week. But the problem was, we always managed to get a lift down there, because it was in the middle of nowhere, but we never found it easy to get back. We told the radio owner our problem – and he told us we could stay later if we liked, as there was no one on after us until 8 a.m. in the morning. So that is what we started doing, a crazy 8 p.m. to 8 a.m. shift. It was a mission, but just goes to show how many hours you can put in when you are doing something you enjoy.

It was fun, but I'd be so tired by the end I was pretty much falling asleep standing up while still talking. I'd run out of people to big up, and by 7 a.m. I'd be saying things as ridiculous as, 'Big up to Maggie Thatcher. Yeah. Big up to John Major.'

I wrote some songs at the time as well, while we were there through the night, and one of them was about Aisha and how I felt about her. I was really proud of that one and recorded it on my iPod. I still have the original notes where I wrote it out, and who knows, I might even bring it out one of these days and release it! I played it to my mate Danny Dyer recently, and he was like, 'Fuck off, that ain't you. It sounds professional; if I heard it on the radio I would turn that up.'

Back on my welding course, though, I was finding things difficult. On the one hand I liked it – welding is a lot more artistic than I had imagined. You can be quite creative and think around things in a way that I enjoy. It's not just about getting a bit of metal and gluing it to another bit of metal; there is a real skill to doing it well and making it look good at the same time. But I was struggling on the maths side of it. You have to draw up plans for what you are going to do, and they can get pretty technical. My brain just shut down and refused to do that section of it. Twice a week we had to do a session of maths drawing, and I got more and more confused and angry with it, as I knew it was letting me down, and making me do a bad job of what I was actually doing really well on every other level. So although I was enjoying the welding, I was struggling too, and I don't respond well to that.

At the same time Dad had stuck to his word about having me down working for his firm on the docks one day a week.

The only job I'd had before this had been brief. At school we had to do work experience, and I went to a place called J & R Belts, just around the corner from my house. It was a small shop that made belts of just about any kind, from clothing belts to car belts, where the bit that looks like a rubber band goes around the engine. I didn't mind it in there too much, and as I had given up hope of ever getting a Saturday job – there were fuck all going around our area – I asked if I could stay on and work for them on Saturdays for a bit of money. I thought it would be good if I could get some of my own money together for once, rather than always depending on Mum. So I was there for a few Saturdays, but the same old problems soon kicked in for me. As soon as they asked me to start making tea for them I couldn't handle it. It went against everything in me – I was a man, and men shouldn't have to be making tea for everyone! It was my old problem of not taking well to authority. And straight away I was out of there.

So I was wary about working for my dad, but at the same time I was looking forward to it. This was my chance to put into action what I was learning at college and prove what I could do, and hopefully make my dad proud in the process. I would head down there at 8 a.m. every Saturday and work my arse off. But I soon found out I wasn't there to do any welding. My dad's attitude was that you start at the bottom and work your way up – the real thinking of a grafter. So I was on the bottom rung for duties. Instead of making these great metal creations, I was sweeping the yard, gathering up bits of scrap metal and wheeling them to the bins. And I was doing jobs like that all day long until 5 or 6 p.m. It was horrible graft, and I know that is everyday life for a lot of people, but it just isn't me. I'm a slight build and a bit of a girly boy, plus I am more creative minded. I'm just not very good at hard manual labour, no matter how much I try. I'm not one of these strapping lads who has the energy and power to spend all day lugging heavy things around.

If I was lucky, the one job I was allowed to do that was a step up was helping to paint. Because the business was making signs, there was a lot of painting to do, but while this was easier than the manual work I didn't like it and had no interest in it at all. I was getting impatient and frustrated – it was welding that I was learning to do as a trade, so I wanted to be having a go at that. I wanted to use my day on the job actually putting into practise what I was learning. But I wasn't getting the chance.

So, between not liking what I was seeing down at the docks with my dad, and struggling with the maths side of the welding course, I was in a dilemma. I knew how disappointed Dad would be, but then I thought, 'Do I really have to do a job I don't want to do, just to try and make my dad love me?' I knew how crazy that sounded, so I dropped the course. It might seem bad, trying out three courses and not following through with any of them, but that's how it was. I've never had the patience to sit through something once I know it is not for me.

Dad was gutted when I told him I was quitting the course, but I think deep down he knew I was right, and that I'm not the same as him or Daniel, and so he didn't give me too much grief over it. I carried on doing one day a week for Dad for a while, just to keep a bit of cash coming in, but after a while I quit that too.

And that was it. I was back to square one, except this time a bit older, at seventeen. I was jobless, penniless, with no real aim in life, living at home with my mum, just the two of us, and really not having a clue what the future would hold.

People around me were starting to sign on, but that wasn't something I wanted to do. Although I was like every other boy on the estate, I still had this idea that I was going to get out of there, and I knew signing on wouldn't help me do that. I could see my older mates who had signed on, and it wasn't good for them. Once they did that, any plans they might have had to get a job went straight out the window. Why would they want a job, when they got more money from benefits than they would if they were paid minimum wage? So I thought I could do better, and I wanted to keep myself on the lookout for work instead.

At least that was the plan – it took a while to become reality. In fact, the next few months of my life I'm not proud of. I just kind of wasted them away, hanging around, getting into fights, smoking joints with my mates, and generally being a nuisance and a layabout. Then things started to get messy, although the start of it wasn't my fault.

I was walking down the street one day when I got stopped by a group of six lads. I knew them from around the place, and knew they were not people to mess with.

'Did you hit my mate the other day?' one of them asked me, while the rest gathered round.

The thing was, I hadn't, but I knew who he was talking about, and it was a friend of mine who had attacked his mate. So I told him that, trying to sound cocky and confident. 'I didn't, but a mate of mine did.'

He came closer to me, looking all threatening, and got into my face. I knew I had to look like I wasn't intimidated.

'Don't fucking give me all that, mate,' I said. 'It weren't nothing to do with me. Fuck off now!'

But he didn't. Instead he lifted his fist and went to punch me, to see if I would flinch, but I didn't. I held still, then carried on my attempt at hard talk. 'Why are you making out to hit me, mate? Either do it or fuck off! Let's face it, there are six of you, and one of me, you'll fucking kill me, but it hardly makes you seem very hard, does it? If you want a proper fight, let me bring a couple of mates of mine to watch my back, and we will have a one on one.'

'All right, do that,' he said. 'See you back here in an hour.'

None of us knew how much it was going to escalate. I thought it was going to be a scary fight, but just one on one. I didn't want to do it, but I knew it was the only chance I had of surviving. Duck out of it, and I'd be beaten twice as badly next time they saw me in the street.

So I rang a couple of older pals, and asked them to come down and watch my back, and told them I wanted no trouble. Well, they only turned up with about twenty or thirty other lads! It felt like they had brought half of Grays with them. I thought,

'Oh God, this has trouble written all over it, I need to wind this up!' but I didn't know how. The best I could do was beg them to let me have my one on one with this geezer, and leave it at that, which they promised.

Of course, it didn't work out that way. Before I even had a chance to say anything to the guy waiting to fight me, the lot behind me just ran at him and his mates. I don't really want to go into detail, but it turned into a huge fight that became brutal and vicious. I won't pretend I didn't join in, of course I did – I had to. Besides, it was these boys who had started it with me earlier in the day. And by the time it ended I remember I was in a white tracksuit that was totally covered in blood, some of it my own from a cut on my face, some other people's. I ran home and through the front door in tears, not knowing what to do.

I burst in and Mum just looked at me in shock.

'Mum, what do I do? I don't want to get in trouble, but what do I do? It was horrible!'

'Give me your clothes, get in the bath, and breathe,' was all she said. So that's what I did.

About an hour later I was on the sofa, just about getting my thoughts together. I was working through what the hell had happened, trying to see if there was any way I could have stopped it. I was shaky from the adrenalin, and freaked out by what I'd just been through. What the hell kind of life was I living? I knew I needed to get out of Grays.

Then there was a heavy knock at the door, and I felt ill. 'Fuck, that's got to be the police,' I thought. And both Mum and

I went to answer it. Well, things were only getting worse. There were ten lads outside my door, all armed with weapons – cricket bats and all sorts. I shit myself, but I'm not one to show it in those situations. Instead I could feel myself getting angry. But before I could say or do anything, my mum beat me to it! She leapt in front of me and started shouting at the lads. 'Leave my fucking son alone! Piss off before you have me to deal with, you hear me?'

You had to see it to believe it. She is as brave as they come, and when she is feeling feisty . . . well, watch out! But I was seventeen, and much as I appreciated the attempt, it hardly made me look good. So I said, 'Mum, get in the house and shut the door. Just watch through the window to make sure nothing too bad happens to me.'

And she did, and I stood there on my own, thinking, I'm getting fucked. I had no idea what to do. So I tried to take the upper hand. 'Right, boys, what do you want?'

'Well, our mate's been beaten up, so what do you think?'

'You started on me when I was on my own, so I had to defend myself. It's over. If you fuck me up now, you know this is only going to get worse.'

But let's face it, reasoning wasn't going to stop them. I was just buying myself time in case a miracle happened. And then it did, in the form of my two friends from the off licence round the corner, who just happened to walk by. They loved me, and I had known them for years, and they always looked out for Mum and me. 'Our little Kirk and Julie from round the way,' they used to call us, when we popped in to get my mum a drink. But while they were nice to us, they were scary geezers in their late twenties, who made our seventeen-year-old really serious fight look like a joke.

'What's going on here, Kirk?' they asked. And as soon as they realized, they told the boys, 'Fuck off, and if anything happens to Kirk, we're gonna do ya!'

And so the lads left, although not without giving me some dirty looks, and that was the problem solved – for the time being. I knew they were never going to just accept that they needed to leave me alone. Instead I started hearing through the grapevine that they were plotting to get me, which put me on edge, and made me more careful about going out on my own. I knew it was only going to be a matter of time.

NINE

A Father and Son Reunion

As a surprise for my eighteenth, my dad sorted out a meal for me. He picked Daniel and me up in a limo along with his family, and we went to London: to The Ivy restaurant. The Ivy! I couldn't believe that I was going from Grays to that – I had never eaten in a place so posh in my life. And if I needed proof that it was where all the celebs went, Kate Moss was there, sitting at the next table, which was insane. That night Dad and I got on better than we ever had. It was because I was now eighteen – he started treating me like a man, and talking to me like I was one, and it felt right.

But his real present to me wasn't the trip to the restaurant – he told me about it in the car on the way there, and it's the best pressie I have ever had.

When everyone was busy in their own conversations, he said to me, 'Kirk, what do you want for your eighteenth? You're a man now but you ain't got nothing to show for it. Your brother is qualified, working and living by himself – you need to sort yourself out.'

'Well, Dad, give me a flat as well, then,' I said, chancing my luck that what he had done for Daniel he might do for me, even though I wasn't working for him. 'I need to get out of this area or I'll end up in proper trouble. I need a place in another town.'

'You can't look after yourself, Kirk, that's a stupid idea,' he said.

'No!' I replied. 'Trust me, Mum is never in as she is working so hard, so I cook and clean for myself all the time!'

'OK, Kirk,' he said, 'I'll go into an agreement with you. I can't just let you have a house, but we can make a deal. Daniel's about to move out of his flat so I'll give it to you. All you've got to do is get a job. I don't care where your job is, just get yourself a job and make sure you have some kind of an income. As long as you've got money to pay your bills and your food shopping, get yourself to work, and the rest of that, I'll give you the flat and pay for everything there. But the minute you get sacked, I'll chuck you out of it and you'll be out on the street like that.'

'Deal!' I shouted, proper excited.

Then it was just a case of finding that job. Dad had a mate called Andy Walker, a great guy who has been around in my life for years – close enough that I call him Uncle Andy. Despite being as mad as a hatter, he has a good insight into people. He will really stick up for me when he thinks I'm right, but when he doesn't, he'll tell me straight, 'Oi, you are pissing your dad off! Sort it out now and be good.' And it works on me every time.

Andy knew I was looking for a job and was keen to see that my deal with my dad happened. He knew a woman who ran a clothes shop in Lakeside and he put me forward for the role, and I got it! It was only serving customers behind the till, but it was a start. I can't say I loved doing the actual job, as it was pretty boring, but what I did like was being able to say I had a job, and people knowing I had a wage. I think until then I had been seen as a bit of a no hoper, especially by Dad and his side of the family. Although they loved me, they looked down on me a bit, because not only had I not had a job until then, I hadn't even had an idea of what I might want to do. So once I had a job, well, they were impressed and pleased with me.

That aside, I knew I needed to get out of my life in Grays. If I stayed I would get in another fight – I might even end up killing someone, or get killed myself. And if I was lucky enough to survive, if I didn't sort myself out I was going to end up as a drug dealer, as there were no other options. As soon as I started that job, Dad stuck to his word and gave me the flat. It was on the outskirts of Grays in Badger's Dene, one of the nicer areas, and was over two floors, with the whole of the top floor, which had originally been the loft, turned into an amazing bedroom. On the day I moved in Dad took me out and bought me everything I needed to set me up, like a microwave and an ironing board. Then it was down to me.

Because of that, I owe everything to him, as he really did save my life. He might not always have been there when I was a kid, and up to the age of eighteen, I definitely owe everything to my mum. But then my dad gave me a chance in life, took me out of Grays, and I love him for that. I might sound soft saying it, but it does bring a tear to my eye even now thinking that he did that for me.

And I think it worked just the way he meant it to, because moving into that house is when I really did grow up. I don't mean all the crazy things I had done when I was younger, trying to prove I was a man – I mean I started to act like one for real. I was taking my job seriously, turning up on time and working hard, then when I got home I was cooking for myself and cleaning the place. It was the start of a whole new life.

After I had been in the clothes shop in Lakeside for about six months, Dad bought this amazing big house on a farm in a nearby village called Bulphan, for him, Stacie and Mason. But there was a lot of work that needed to be done, and as he knew I had been getting bored in the shop, he told me to come and work at the farm as a labourer, helping out on the building. The plan was to completely redo the big house, so we built a little house on the grounds as well, for the three of them to live in while we were working on the bigger one.

By now Dad and I were getting on a lot better, but I still could never say that we were really close. There was always a barrier between us that I could never put my finger on, but I was pretty sure Stacie had something to do with it.

Then Christmas 2006 came around. As I said before, I never enjoyed Christmas at my Dad's because it was always uncomfortable, and by now Stacie and I didn't even want to be in the same room. But this year was particularly bad, especially Christmas dinner, because it was obvious the problem wasn't just between me and Stacie – she and Dad seemed to have fallen out too. She was heavily pregnant with their second child, by then, but no one was talking; not one word was spoken through the whole meal. It was the worst Christmas ever. I'd rather have sat in the house with no electricity with my mum, like we had done all those years before, than go through that day.

So we stayed until Boxing Day and then Dad dropped me at Mum's house. I don't know all the ins and outs of what happened, but I think Dad went home and Stacie had gone to her parents', so he decided to go out. When he got home at 2 a.m. Stacie had bagged up all his belongings and their relationship was over.

He called me the next day and said, 'Hi, Kirk, do you want to come around mine?'

'Not really,' I replied honestly. 'We just sat there and Stacie didn't want to speak to us. I hardly wanna come back to that.'

'Stacie's left. It is just me.'

'What? What's happening?'

'Stacie's gone for good. She got the hump and we're over.'

Instead he gave me his new address – luckily one of his rental homes, a flat, was free so he was staying there – and I popped round. And that was it. Things changed from that minute, and I suddenly got back the dad I had always wanted.

He said, 'Right, Kirk, I gotta kit out this new place of mine. Do you wanna go to Ikea with me and help me get stuff?'

And we went and bought everything to make it a proper place, and spent the next two days putting it all together – the bookcases, TV stand, cupboards, the lot. And sometimes we chatted about all sorts of things, and other times we just worked next to each other in silence, but the whole time I could feel our bond growing. Everything I imagined other kids felt about their dads when they were hanging out together, I started to feel for the first time in those two days.

And it didn't stop with the house being kitted out. I was with him all the time from then on. His place was really close to mine, so I could walk there in no time, and I'd go round while he was at work and sort things out for him. He'd call me up and say, 'Kirk, do you mind taking those clothes to the laundrette for me?'

Or I would ring him. 'Dad, what time are you going to be home from work? I was gonna make us dinner.'

And I'd get it all prepared for when he came in. I really liked doing these things, because I could, and I loved that he needed me to do stuff for him. Then afterwards we would watch a movie or something, and I'm not embarrassed to say, I would cuddle up to him while we watched it. It was like the little boy in me, who hadn't got the cuddles off my dad when I was younger, was making up for the lost time.

Other days we would go shopping at Lakeside, or just chill out, heading to the cinema or the pub. He started getting me to hang out with him and his mates, and I was one of the boys. He was letting me into a part of his life that I had never been involved with before. We were like best mates, and we hardly left each other's side.

Even my mum, who you might think wouldn't have been happy about it, who might have resented her 'mummy's boy' suddenly spending so much time with the man who had left our family, was really pleased for us. I am sure a part of her found it hard when I would say, 'Oh sorry, Mum, I can't see you tonight, I'm off to see Dad.' But she kept it well hidden. She knew growing up it was the thing in my life that used to make me cry the most, Dad not really being in my life. She was the one who had heard me crying myself to sleep when I was little, and when she asked, 'What's up?' I told her, 'I want a dad. I want my dad! I just want him to love me.' I know it broke her heart, so for things to be sorting themselves out, even if it was fourteen years late, was still better than nothing. When I came home with a smile on my face she would tell me, 'I'm proud of you, Kirk. I'm glad you're getting on with your dad.'

I get upset even writing this. She was so lovely and understanding, and tried so hard all my life. I didn't even realize how hard things might have been for her, mentally, physically and financially, until I started writing them down in this book.

Around this time, Dad really started splashing the cash on me.

He'd say, 'Here, Kirk, do you want a new watch? This five-grand Cartier one is really nice, I'll buy it for you.'

Or, 'Here's two grand – go and do a bit of clothes shopping, you need some new outfits.'

I'd suddenly gone from having fuck all money, and I really do mean fuck all, to having thousands of pounds. And I was spending it so fast, I didn't really grasp the value of it. When I passed my driving test, it was crazy. Just before I went in for it, Dad said, 'What car do you want if you pass, Kirk? I have to buy you your first car.'

I wanted a Renault Clio.

'You're not having one of them, they're shit! What do you really want?'

'That's all I want, Dad. That, or a Peugeot 206.'

And he laughed and went off and bought me a Range Rover. A Range Rover for my first car! I was so grateful, but the down-side is that when you start with a top-of-the-range car, you are never going to want anything less.

Another time he asked Daniel and me, 'Do you want to come on holiday with me and me mates?'

'Are you fucking serious?!'

'Yeah, come on, we're off to Ibiza. I'll pay for it all, so you don't need to worry about anything.'

And off we went, and had a great holiday with him. Apart from a trip to Minorca that we had taken as a family when he and my mum had still been together, which I couldn't even remember, this was the first time I had been away with him. It was our first proper holiday, and I loved it. He was becoming like my best mate. I was only gutted that there was no way to get Mum involved, and there were times lying on the sun lounger in the grounds of our private villa when I had a real knot of guilt in my stomach, thinking of her sat at home alone in a grotty council flat.

Back in the UK, Dad moved out of the flat he had been stay-ing in temporarily, and bought himself a massive house in Benfleet with a games room and an indoor swimming pool. But I was still seeing him just as much.

Meanwhile, Stacie had given birth to their second kid, a girl named Hollie, and Dad was getting access to both her and

Mason. He moved her into a proper lovely new place, and at the same time got me to move to the small house on the farm to keep an eye on the last bit of the work being done there. It was a gorgeous house, and so big just for me on my own. I fell in love with it straight away. It is where I still live today, and is the house I described at the beginning of this book. But I felt guilty as well. I'm not lying when I say my games room is bigger than my mum's flat. Even Dad's dog kennel is nearly as big, because those dogs are spoilt – they have a proper heated house!

Then Dad started really getting into going out, especially to this one club in Brentwood High Street called Sugar Hut. It was a pretty ordinary club that was one of the places to go at the time. He would head there with his mate Andy Walker, who had got me the job in Lakeside, and some other men. Some evenings he'd call me up and say, 'Kirk, come and get ready with the boys,' and we would all go round to Dad's house before we went out, and make a real boys' night of it. Although I was the youngest, I didn't feel like I shouldn't have been there. I have always been mature for my age, and I was able to get on with them easily and fit in.

Sometimes Daniel was there and he would come too, but he had moved to Malia, in Crete, to teach diving, and he was travelling as well, so he wasn't around as much.

I also enjoyed trying to get Dad to change his appearance. At this time he was very overweight – about nineteen stone – wore glasses, was so pale it looked like he had never seen sunshine in his life, and he was a skinhead. His clothes were a bit ropey too – he just wasn't a looker. So I said to him, 'Dad, you're single now – get some new clothes, keep your hair short on the sides and let it grow longer on the top, start using a bit of gel and take a bit of pride in how you look. It's time to start making yourself look good!'

We went shopping to Lakeside and got him a whole new wardrobe of good designer clothes. I even convinced him it was time to try a sunbed. I had only started going on them myself the odd time, but realized how much better I looked afterwards. It wasn't something I would have done growing up in Grays! But in the new world I was starting to move in, it was a lot more common. Never a spray tan, mind you – that is more something for girls – but a sunbed was good for me. Dad wasn't happy about it at first, but then he really got into it. I loved helping him with his image and soon he was a different man!

And wow, did he love Sugar Hut, and did they love him in there . . . He was their biggest spender – I'm sure he was splashing out £5,000 to £10,000 a night, and he would be in there three nights a week. We'd go in, and Dad would get the guy behind the bar and hand over £5,000, and tell him, 'Let me know when that's run out.' And everyone on our table would be drinking champagne and vodka, and whatever else, all on Dad.

At first, I loved it. Sugar Hut was really nice – much more glamorous than the places I was used to going to. But mostly it was about Dad. He was so popular, it was untrue. All these young birds would be coming over to hang out with us, and I couldn't believe they were there to chat my dad up. I wanted him to meet a new girl – of course I did. I hadn't liked Stacie because I blamed her for splitting my family up, whereas now

Dad could start from scratch with someone totally different who could make him happy. I wanted him to settle down again, but I hoped it wouldn't be with one of the Sugar Hut lot, as they weren't around him for the right reasons – they liked his money, and were looking for a sugar daddy type of boyfriend. Dad has quite a tough image as well, and that always attracts the girls. So while I was happy to see him have fun – and I knew it was great for his ego to get the attention – I didn't want him getting serious with any of them.

I loved hanging out with him because his kudos rubbed off on me – people who wouldn't have noticed me before started paying me attention. And my dad was proud of me. If he was chatting to a girl he would always be sure to wave me over, saying, 'Here, let me introduce you to my son.'

Until that time, part of me had always thought he gave me attention because he had to, because we were related by blood. But for the first time, I realized he was seeing me not because he had to, but because he wanted to. And that while I mightn't have given him that many reasons to be proud of me in life, he didn't hate me, and he wanted everyone to see we were hanging out together – in fact, he was bragging about it!

Dad never once apologized for leaving Daniel and me, or for the crap we went through as kids because of him. But in a way, it felt like he was going out of his way now to make up for it. He had become my biggest idol, my David Beckham. Kids look up to David; I looked up to my dad. No longer just for his business mind – the bit that had fascinated me as a kid – but for everything he did. He had become an all-round hero for me.

But the problem was, I was starting to get spoilt. For the first few months I had been shocked by the way he threw money around, and there were times I would look at him paying one night's bar tab, and think, 'Wow, Mum could pretty much live off that for a year!' It wasn't a good feeling, and resentment that he wasn't helping her would once again well up in me. When I could, I'd pass some cash on to her. If he gave me money to shop for myself, for example, I'd try to get her something new as well, or I'd go round and give her a whole bundle of notes, to do with whatever she wanted.

But without me realizing it, the money and other things that Dad gave me were starting to become normal. I was getting through the cash without really appreciating it, and just expected more of it to keep coming. People have accused me of living off my dad, which is simply not true. However, the reality was that between the ages of eighteen and nineteen, I did. Then again, I was hardly going to say no to all these offers, was I?

Once I turned nineteen, things changed. Suddenly he started to refuse me money. I remember saying, 'Dad, can I have a new watch for my birthday?' And I pointed out the new Cartier one.

And he laughed, and said, 'Who the fuck do you think you are? You ain't me, stop trying to be so flash!'

The same happened when I asked him to pay for a holiday. 'Dad, can I have some money for a holiday?'

'Pay for your own holiday,' was all he said.

'What?' I couldn't believe what I was hearing.

'No, you've had your year now, mate,' he told me. 'You gotta look after yourself. You gotta stand on your own two feet.'

And while I understood what he meant on one level, I was mad on another. Until the big fight had turned things sour, I had been quite happy in my poor life in Grays, because I had never known anything different. Now he had brought me into a new lifestyle, full of money, cars and expensive designer goods, then moaned when I wanted help to stay in it. It made me wonder if I might have done better staying in my old life in a way, as that had been normal to me when I was in it. But to go back to it now would have been really difficult.

Then Dad got a girlfriend who wasn't much older than I was. She worked in a strip club, and he asked her to leave her job and be his girlfriend. Suddenly it seemed as if he was starting to pull away from me. I'd ring and ask, 'Dad, do you wanna go to the cinema tonight?'

'Nah, mate, I'm not in the mood tonight.'

Then I'd find out later that he had gone to see a film with his girlfriend instead. And little things like that kept happening. I know it sounds daft to be jealous, but I felt myself starting to panic, like I was losing him to a woman all over again. All the feelings I'd had when he was with Stacie kept coming back, and I could see our closeness slipping away. I felt scared and upset, and angry all at the same time.

To be honest, deep down I think I am an insecure person – when it comes to my dad, especially, I'm pretty emotionally vulnerable. Now I felt like I was falling down his priority list, and I didn't like it one little bit.

TEN

Sugar Hut

Then one day, out of the blue, Dad told me he was buying half of Sugar Hut. It was mad. One week we were customers, then the next, he owned half the place. I guess he must have liked what he saw, because not long after, he bought the whole thing.

I was at a bit of a loose end, job-wise. We had finished most of the work on his house, and I was looking around for other labouring to do. But instead Dad asked me to go and work at Sugar Hut for him, which I thought sounded good. I started going down all the time and helping out. But I'll be honest, I have very mixed up feelings about him buying Sugar Hut. Sometimes I think it was the worst career and lifestyle move he has ever made, while other times I love that place and everything that comes with it.

What I didn't like, though, was the difference I was seeing in Dad. I felt like he really changed as a person. All the smaller things I had noticed before became bigger. We're similar, in that we both get really sucked into whatever we are doing, and he

161

got really sucked into that club, and the lifestyle. Everyone was hanging around him, kissing his arse, while milking him at the same time. They would be telling him, 'Mick, you're the man,' and he'd think they were genuine, and I hated it. Before I'd thought it was cool to have all these young girls hanging around him, but now it just seemed like they wanted to use him, and I didn't like it.

When he first bought it, Sugar Hut wasn't doing particularly well. It needed a lot of work to turn it around, and so Dad sold his businesses and a lot of his properties to finance that. At first it was a real drain on his money, and it worried me.

But on the other hand, I did love it. I loved the social thing, and that so many people in Brentwood knew who I was. I had gone from being this little scally kid from the wrong side of Essex to someone people wanted to be associated with. And, more importantly, two great things came out of those early months in Sugar Hut for me – Dappy, and Amy Childs.

Even though N-Dubz were only just starting to slip into the public's awareness in 2007, I had been following their career for a long time and was a massive fan. I loved what they were doing, and thought all three of them, Dappy, Fazer and Tulisa, were really talented. So I was proper chuffed for them when they won Best Newcomer at the MOBO Awards in September that year. We were hosting the after-party at Sugar Hut, and I wasn't supposed to be working that night, but I told my mates, 'If N-Dubz come to the party, text me, 'cos I will be there fast as anything!'

And of course I got a text: 'All three of them are here, get your arse down!'

So I raced to the club, and then as soon as I got there I thought, 'Shit, what do I do now?' I was like a proper fan, and didn't know how to start talking to them, even though I was desperate to. In the end I just got a bottle of our best champagne and went over to their table. I was shaking and everything!

'Congratulations on the award, guys,' I said. 'My dad owns this place, and we wanted to send this over on the house to say well done, and we're really happy to have you in here.'

'Nice one, bruv,' said Dappy. 'But we're only drinking it if you sit with us and help us out.'

So I did, and that was the start of our friendship. All three of them are sound, but it was Dappy who I really clicked with. We are from similar backgrounds and had both been thrown into money, and were learning to enjoy the lifestyle that comes with cash, without losing touch with our roots. We are also like each other in that we say what we think – sometimes too much!

After that night we kept in touch. We don't meet up that often – music is Dappy's priority in life, and he is away all around the world a lot of the time – but we catch up when we can. I go round to his and he'll be there playing with his kids. Despite what people think, he is really good with them, and is a great dad.

I think Dappy has been massively misunderstood over the years. He has a good heart and always does what he thinks is right. Sometimes he just needs a bit of guidance, because his dad passed away just as he was getting famous, and I think he hasn't got that person around any more who could give him a nudge when he is starting to do something a bit wrong without realizing. He always supports me, and I try and do the same for him – even earlier this year when he had to go to court accused of assault and affray over a fight in a petrol station, I went down to the trial to show him I was there for him.

But the absolute best thing to come out of that first year in Sugar Hut, for me, was Amy Childs. I still remember the day I met Amy, when she was introduced to me in the Sugar Hut Restaurant by a mutual friend. She was my ideal type then, and still is now in some ways, and I fell for her on the spot.

She was two years younger than me, so was sixteen, almost seventeen, and had just left school and started at college, studying beauty. She was working at the same time as well, in a salon linked to a Virgin gym. Already she looked like a glamour model, and that is the look I love. I hold my hands up, the faker a girl looks, the more I find her attractive – boob job, pumped-up lips, hair extensions . . .

But it wasn't just her looks that I went for, it was her personality as well. I had such a connection with her – I really felt like she was my soul mate. I didn't connect with many girls at that point, as I still felt awkward around them, but Amy was different; it was like she was the female version of me. I was instantly relaxed with her, as though we were brother and sister, but there was this huge chemistry there as well. She was just brilliant and so perfect. It was like we were made for each other, and from that first day, we were proper close.

We'd spend loads of time together – she became a regular in the club, and we were always round each other's houses. And we'd just sit and talk for hours. People always think Amy is really dippy, and it's true – she is as dippy as anything! But when she wants to be clever about something, she can really put her mind to it. There is a sharpness there that not everyone sees, but believe me, it is there.

And it helped that I loved her family to bits – they became like my second family. I'd go round and her mum would say, 'Oh, sorry, Kirk, Amy isn't in.'

'That's fine, I'll come in and see you!'

And Amy's mum and I would catch up over a cuppa.

Since Aisha I'd had my fair share of flings, but I hadn't had a proper girlfriend. And now what I felt for Amy made me realize that Aisha had been more like a schoolboy crush. But my feelings are hard to explain. While a bit of me knew it was love, a bit of me was fighting it as well. Dad now owned the most popular club in Essex, I was getting loads of attention from stunning girls and I didn't really want to get tied down! It was like I had met her at the worst time.

And Amy felt a similar way. Both of us were huge flirts, but also hugely jealous of each other, so we'd kick off if we saw the other one getting close to someone else in the bar. It was like there was a constant power struggle between us. One person would be fighting for the other, and more in love, and then it would switch. So we were on and off a lot, but there was a connection that kept pulling me back to her.

As for my actual role in Sugar Hut, well, it wasn't very defined at first. I was running around doing a bit of nothing and everything, just helping anyone who needed it. I enjoyed being there, but I didn't feel like I had really got my position in the club sorted, and I was still looking round for something to focus on, so I could make my mark. Daniel had come to work at Sugar Hut as well, because obviously with Dad selling the welding businesses, he had to have a rethink when he got back from abroad, and Dad had asked him to come and work there instead.

Then I was in the club one Thursday night, and Dad was about to close the place early as it was pretty empty. Although Thursdays seemed to work really well in central London, out in Essex they were dead. No one ever went out on a Thursday. So I stood there thinking . . . could I be the one to change that? This could be the kind of challenge I needed, something for me to take on and prove myself.

'Dad . . .' I went over to see him, already sure he would knock me down, but determined to try. 'I know I'm not a pro- moter, and I've never done it before in my life, but how would you feel about me taking over Thursday nights and seeing if there is anything I can do with them?'

'Not a fucking chance, mate,' he told me straight off. 'You ain't got a clue about running a night. Forget it!'

But I wasn't willing to give up. 'You have nothing to lose, Dad!' I told him. 'We're closing tonight 'cos it's so dead, and I'm the same age as the people you're trying to pull in, so maybe I'll have a chance. Just give me a go, just a couple of months, and see if I can turn it around. It won't cost ya, I just wanna try. Come on!'

In the end, he probably just thought he would get an easier ride if he let me get stuck in. And that is exactly what I did. I grafted my arse off on that night. I thought of a name for it, booked in a DJ who played the type of music everyone in the area liked (not MC'ing, by the way – I had sacked that off by then!), had nice flyers printed up, then handed them out myself, visiting every shop in the area.

Then on the night I made sure it was perfectly run inside, and would go round myself seeing that everyone was having a good time, and if not, what I could do to change it. I made it my dream club night, and because I was a typical Essex teen, it was perfect for the crowd we were trying to pull in.

In the end, I put Thursdays on the map in Essex. It became the biggest night at Sugar Hut, much bigger than Fridays or Saturdays – but, more importantly, I had found my niche in life. I had discovered something I was really good at – promotion and marketing. Finally, after all the dropped college courses, and hours spent telling people I didn't know what I wanted to do, I had a direction.

I even had a bongo player going along with the DJ, which I loved, and I started to get good on the bongos myself. Whenever Dad was in the club he would make me get up and join in – he liked that, and it was another of those times when I could see the pride in his eyes.

Even though Dad would obviously never allow Mum into the club, I would still go round to see her all the time. I was – and still am – as much of a mummy's boy as ever, and it was important to me to tell her about my life. I wanted to make sure she was still proud of me. She has always told me she is, even when I was being the worst little shit in the world, but it was still good to hear it.

I'd talk to her about everything else in my life, too, like friends, and girls, and get her advice on things. She has always kept me grounded, and not let the lifestyle go to my head. Mum is a reminder of my roots, and who I am. The only thing I tried not to talk to her about much was anything that seemed like I was showing off my money. I was even embarrassed driving up to her flat in my latest car – Dad got us to keep changing them every six months or so, as he has a car dealer mate, so I always have something that is really new. But when I was there I would always try and pass on some of the money that I had kept back for her.

I was loving my life at that time: club, money, girls and success – it all seemed to be going the right way. Then one evening I booked Brian Belo for a PA on my night. He had won *Big Brother* 2007, and as he is from Essex, I was sure he would be a great pull for a Thursday night crowd – everyone in our area is always proud of a local boy done good.

So Brian came down and was a massive success, but not only that, I found a new friend. We got on really well. He was a lot like me, too, as he'd gone from having no money to having a load – him through a TV show, me through my dad – and he was struggling to deal with it, while still sticking to his roots and remaining the guy he knew he was. We started hanging out and I would go round to his house – he had a great mum who was totally focused on him and his family, and who reminded me of my own mum.

I brought him to the club all the time, originally as a pull, but then that became irrelevant – I wanted him down there as a mate. We would spend hours chatting, and I really trusted the guy.

One evening we were chilling in Sugar Hut, and he said to me, 'Kirk, I love this money, this club, this lifestyle. I keep having an idea for a TV show, but I just don't know if it'll work.'

'Go on, try me – what do you mean?'

'What do you think if we filmed what we're doing? I think people would want to see it, to see this Essex lifestyle. Do you not think it would be a laugh?'

I thought it might be funny to give it a go, so I said, 'Yeah, why not?' and we discussed who would be good people in the area to follow as part of the show, characters who were popular and very Essex. He knew Mark Wright and said he thought he would be good, and I suggested Amy, of course! I wasn't being biased, though – she was really popular, and summed up what Essex girls – at least the well-off, glam end – were about, and I knew she would be great viewing. I also mentioned Sam Faiers, who was a regular at that club by then, and a school mate of Amy's, and I imagine Mark must have talked about her too, as at that time they were working together at Embassy nightclub, up in London's West End.

So Brian went away and, along with his manager Adam Muddle, organized filming for a pilot for a possible show called *Totally Essex*. For my part, I just had to talk to camera about my money and my lifestyle. I didn't think too much about it at the time, and I didn't expect it to lead to anything – it was more like a bunch of mates messing around with a video camera at home. You can still see the video on YouTube, if you want a laugh!

And that seemed to be the end of it, so I just got on with my normal life. In fact we had something much more pressing to deal with at that time – Sugar Hut caught fire.

It was September 2009. An electrical fault out the back started a blaze, and the structure survived but on the inside the place was completely destroyed. We had to start again from scratch, and the club was shut for eleven months before we got it up and running again.

It really ate into my dad's business. We had just got the club to a place where it was making good money, and then that happened. It was pretty heart-breaking, especially as the insurance company refused to pay out on a technicality. Dad had to put £2 million into revamping the place.

Sugar Hut finally reopened again in August 2010 with a big launch party. We wanted so badly for things to pick up where they had left off the year before, and keep getting stronger. But other clubs had sprung up in the meantime and people's loyalties had changed, so we knew we had our work cut out to get them back. Dad was pumping lots of money into it to get it going, and we were constantly trying to think of ways to make it happen. It put a lot of strain on him, Daniel and me as a family, because we are all very opinionated about the best way to do things, and with the added financial pressure, we were mentally stretched to our limits.

*

About nine months after we had done the pilot with Brian, I got approached about a possible show in Essex, this time by a company called Lime Pictures. It was to be called *The Only Way Is Essex*, and it seemed like this really was going to happen, because these were big bosses, not just a mate of mine who I was having a laugh with. Also, it was being lined up to go on ITV2, which meant this was serious stuff.

At this point I stopped and thought, 'Do I really want to be on TV and be famous?' It was a hard one. I am not someone who has gone looking for fame. In fact being put in front of a crowd of people and being judged is one of my worst nightmares, as I have already said. So to choose to put myself out there, on a national scale, was a genuinely scary idea. But at the same time there was another part of me that did like the idea of being on TV. There must be a bit of us all that would like it – everyone on TV is an inspiration to someone, and I loved the idea of being that person.

But that aside, I wanted to do it to help raise the profile of Sugar Hut. The producers told me they wanted to film me mainly in the club, focusing on my life in there. And as the venue had only just reopened and hadn't really picked up again yet, this seemed like the perfect opportunity for us. We could buy radio adverts, place an ad in the paper, and all of that, but no marketing would do as much as putting the club in a TV show. So that was my main motivation, above all else. And to add that little extra incentive, Dad didn't want to be involved because he was nervous about how the show was going to be perceived, and he was worried about looking shit, so he told me that for *TOWIE* I could pretend that I actually owned the club.

We decided I should go for it. I was going to be one of *TOWIE*'s original founding cast members. But sometimes I think now, if I could turn back time, I would never have done it; I would never be famous in a million years . . .

ELEVEN

The Only Way Is Essex

Filming for the first season of *TOWIE* started in September 2010, and it all felt a bit daft, but a good laugh. We were supposed to just get on with normal life, and then producers would talk to us about what we were up to and choose bits of what we were doing to film. Of course it ended up being storylined in ways that I will explain in a minute, as that made for more entertaining TV.

I was conscious of the cameras when they were there, and I can see now, watching myself in those early episodes, that at the start I did look uncomfortable with them. The crew would sometimes put crosses on the floor where we needed to stand, which makes it easier for the camera crew, and so I would walk along looking at the floor, then stop, and only then lift my head! But I soon got used to it all.

I had got my mum involved in the show, too, as I figured if they wanted the real me, then she was one hundred per cent a part of that. I love looking out for her, and I wanted people not

173

just to see me in the club, but also to see the relationship I have with my mum – how we are there for each other and have a real bond. And viewers did see that – in my very first scene I am pulling up at my mum's house to drop off some shopping for her, and then in my second scene I am talking about Amy with her, and getting her advice on my feelings. And that is how it continues in series one – you see her as my friend, my mum and the person I talk to about everything. And that is exactly how my life was off the camera.

Because TOWIE is filmed with the aim that it is as close in time to real life as possible, I think we had only filmed about two episodes before it hit the screens. And, wow! Despite everything the producers had told us they were hoping for, the reaction was still unbelievable. The first show got over a million viewers when it aired on a Sunday, and I couldn't believe it – I don't think I'd been aware of how much hype there was.

The next morning, going to work as normal, I called in to the bakery across the road from Sugar Hut. The same bakery that I had been going to for a year, every morning, for my breakfast. The same bakery where no one who worked there had ever spoken to me other than to ask my order. Not that Monday morning.

'Kirk! How are you doing?' the guy behind the counter said to me. 'What can we get for you, the usual? Don't worry about queuing, skip it – you are one of our regulars, after all!'

I just looked at them and thought, 'Wow, how shallow are you? Just 'cos I was on TV last night, you're treating me like this.

The fact that I have been a customer for a year doesn't count – one night on the TV, and I'm the best.'

And while other people might have loved it, I hated it. Of course it was a positive in some ways, because I got my breakfast more quickly! But I wasn't comfortable with it, and could feel everyone else in the queue staring at me. The reality was it put a bit of a downer on my first day of TV fame.

One thing I did immediately change after that first episode was the number of sunbeds I was having. Up until that point, I'd only had them now and then, to stop myself looking too pale, but on-screen – well, it wasn't enough! I still looked really pale, especially as everyone else on the show was so tanned. So I started going once a week at least, to get some serious colour going. And after a while the salon started to become a bit of a social thing. Everyone in there knows each other, and now I can hardly ever go without seeing a mate and having a good catch-up with someone!

A lot of my scenes at this stage were with Amy. Although we weren't properly dating when the show started, we were in our usual on/off set-up, where we didn't commit, but still couldn't stay away from each other. The producers saw the potential in the chemistry between us and told us, 'You two are brilliant together, the viewers love it!'

And they weren't lying – they did! We were one of the things about the show that people were discussing more than anything on Twitter, Facebook and other online forums. They really got into the dilemma of my jealousy, and her worrying I wouldn't be faithful to her.

What I didn't know at the time was that Amy was seeing two other guys outside of the show. She loves being spoilt by her boyfriends, and she had these two blokes on the go, both of whom were proper wining and dining and looking after her. They were Joe Hurlock, who she eventually openly dated after we split on the show, and another guy called Ben.

On the other hand, I was single, apart from Amy. By then I actually would have been up for a proper exclusive relationship with her, but she wasn't ready to put in the effort. At the same time, whenever I flirted with anyone in Sugar Hut and it was filmed, I was made out to be the bad person, because no one knew Amy was seeing other people! Amy was very good at getting inside my head and playing with me. I guess because by then I wanted to give things a proper go, she held the upper hand. And she did make me think I was the one for her.

Then she asked me to get a tattoo of her name. I wasn't up for that, but I was already planning to get a tattoo on my leg of Bettie Page, the famous 1950s pin-up girl. So I decided to make it look more like Amy, as a bit of a tribute to her. It was so weird the day I showed it to Amy – she turned up in this red dress, with red shoes and lipstick, and even two gold bangles – exactly like my tattoo!

Amy loved the fact the public thought she was this sweet girl who was being messed around by me, and were really getting on her side. It wasn't fair because I knew what the public didn't — that she wasn't fully committed to me but for the rest of the series Amy and I continued our same crazy on/off relationship. I couldn't stay away from her, but she wasn't prepared to do what was needed to make it a proper relationship either.

So at one point during the first series, when I was sick of Amy leading me on and then going back to the other guys, I knew I had to turn my head away from her. I was talking to one of the extras (ha!!!), Maria Fowler, and I said to her, 'I'm sick of being single. I need to find a nice girl, but someone more mature, not a young girl like Amy who doesn't know how to behave properly.'

She said, 'Well, my mate is looking for someone, so I could set you up with her: Lauren Pope.'

And she looked at me expecting me to know who Lauren was. I didn't, but I asked around a few of my mates, and they did know her – she was famous as a Page Three model as we were growing up, but I hadn't really noticed all that.

So Maria gave me Lauren's number and we started texting. She was older – I was twenty-two at the time and she was twenty-nine – but she sounded like good fun, and we got on well. In true Kirk style I said we should meet up, but then I didn't know what to do for a first date.

'What do you want to do?' I asked her. I was off to do a photoshoot in London the next day, so she said, 'Shall we go to the cinema? I can meet you at the O2 after your shoot and we can go to the cinema there.'

'Good plan,' I said. 'The only problem is if we meet after

my shoot, a car will have picked me up in the morning so I won't be driving. This sounds bad, but do you mind dropping me home after?'

'No, that's fine. Shall I reserve tickets in case it gets sold out?'

And I told her, yes, and that was all good. I went to my shoot, then on to the O2. And I was standing there waiting for her, and I didn't know what she would be like. I had googled her, of course, but no one really looks like their picture. But then she turned up, and I thought, 'Wow!' She was in skinny jeans, a beige jacket and a sexy pair of sunglasses, and she just looked unreal. I was blown away, but I was thinking, 'Fuck, this is definitely going to be our last date, because she's going to take one look at me and I won't be good enough. She looks like a supermodel!'

But we went for a few drinks, and we got on really well. She was great company and we had a laugh, and I instantly felt relaxed with her. Then we went to the cinema, and she picked up our reserved tickets. I was gutted because I hadn't realized her reserving them meant she had paid for them as well, so I felt really bad. We were watching that Facebook film, *The Social Network*, and right at the end, even though she had told me she didn't kiss on the first date, I thought, 'I've got to go for this,' so I did, and she kissed me back, and it all just felt right.

Then she dropped me home. How bad does that sound? I could imagine her friends asking, 'How did your first date go?' And she'd have to say, 'Well, I drove there, I paid for the tickets, then I dropped him home.'

They would have been like, 'Bin him off!' So in one way it

wasn't my ideal first date, but in another way, it was – because she was great.

And then we started seeing each other properly. But of course as Amy and I were still seen together on the show I felt I had to see Lauren in secret, while working things through with Amy. It was all a bit of a mess. I felt as if Amy was TOWIE's princess, and it seemed to me that she dictated what was filmed. But then Amy decided she didn't want to be with me any more on screen anyway, so I said to the producers, 'Can we please bring in Lauren, as she really is my girlfriend, and if this is supposed to be our real lives, she needs to be on it!' They agreed, and after that TOWIE started to feel closer to my real life – as far as my love life went, anyway.

The other big thing for me during that first series of TOWIE was my boxing fight with Mark Wright, which was the biggest load of bollocks, and still makes me angry to this day. Writing about it, I can feel the rage starting to rise up in me again.

Basically, I never had a problem with Mark Wright. I didn't know him before Brian Belo was putting together his pilot, and he invited Mark along to that. I thought he seemed a nice enough lad, and we got along fine. In my opinion, the problem was more on Mark's side, because he wanted what I had. At the time he was a club promoter, whereas my dad owned a club. All club promoters like to think they will own a club one day, that is their ultimate aim. I've never wanted what anyone else has – I've been given my lot and I am happy with it, and I know I am lucky to have it, but not so with Mark.

You could always see his frustration bubbling under the surface because he wasn't the big club person on the show in series one – that was me. So he was constantly being competitive and trying to undermine me – like when he opened Deuces bar and tried to take my staff away, and told me it was a contest between Deuces and Sugar Hut, him and me. I always took it with a pinch of salt, and would just laugh and go along with it. But the TOWIE producers loved it, and were forever putting us in situations that would exaggerate the competition between us. I didn't mind too much at first, as it was just banter, but then it started to become annoying.

One day Mark came over to me, off camera, and said, 'Have you ever boxed before, Kirk?'

'Never in my life, brother,' I told him.

'Well, I'm supposed to be doing this charity boxing match,' he told me. 'But the guy I'm meant to fight, I've heard he's a bit of a boxer, and I ain't got a clue how to box. Can we do it instead – you versus me in the boxing ring? It'll be a good storyline for TOWIE, and we'll have a laugh.'

'Course, mate,' I said. 'Especially if it's for charity.'

So I signed up to do it, and Mark and I agreed not to train or take it too seriously, but just to fight it out on the day, and we discussed it on camera so that people would know about it. And every day Mark would call me up and say, 'You ain't training, are you, Kirk?'

And I told him, 'Apart from jogging every day to get my stamina up, as I know you're a footballer, no, I'm not.'

'Thing is,' he said, sounding worried, 'everyone keeps telling me you can fight, and I haven't had any time to train.'

'The only fights I've ever had have been on the street, mate. I haven't got a clue how to box, so stop worrying!' I promised him.

And I meant it. I didn't know how to box properly. The only time I had set foot in a ring before my fight with Mark was when I had a lesson with a cage fighter, which was filmed for *TOWIE* as a bit of a laugh. It was a three-minute scene and that was all the training advice I'd ever had!

The day before the fight, Mark went to see my dad and pulled him into the office.

'Mick,' he said. 'I'm a bit worried. I know Kirk is a bit of a live wire, and I don't know how to fight. This is only a bit of fun for charity, and I want Kirk to remember that. Can you remind Kirk it is only for TV so not to go in the ring all guns blazing?'

So Dad called me up and said, 'Look, Kirk, don't do what you normally do and go mad, 'cos Mark's a bit scared. Pace yourself with him.'

And I felt bad that Mark was worrying, and said of course I'd take it easy.

The morning of the fight I got to the venue – the City Pavilion in Romford – and found the headgear that had been sorted out for me. Then when I went to say 'hi' to Mark, he didn't want to talk to me. He was trying to be the man and psych himself up, and psych me out. But even then, fucking stupid me didn't clock what was happening. I felt sorry for him as I thought he must be shitting himself and this was all part of his act. I'll be honest, I thought I had it in the bag. I thought it would be a bit of a light-hearted spar, and when it came down to it, I would easily win.

So I got in the ring first, then he made his entrance and proper squared up to me, all aggressive. But what I was really noticing was his headgear. While I'd been given one that went above my eyebrows and past my ears and left my whole face uncovered, he had got one that came under his eyebrows and covered his cheekbones, jaws, the lot. There was practically no way to punch his face with that on! But I thought, well, it doesn't matter too much. If he doesn't know how to fight, I will still win.

Then the bell went, and bang! First punch, Mark broke my nose, then bang, bang, bang, he was straight in there smashing me again! My helmet split and I couldn't see, so they had to pause the fight.

Back in my corner, my man told me, 'He is a proper boxer, mate. You've been had!'

I went back out there and swung like mad and took him to the floor. But I was shaken from the start, my helmet was falling in my eyes every two seconds and I could hardly see to fight back. I was covered in blood, disorientated and so angry I couldn't think straight. The fight went to the full three rounds, and by the end I looked a mess and Mark was judged to be the winner.

Afterwards I found out that Mark has been boxing since he was four. His dad was an amateur boxer, and his granddad Eddy was a professional. Boxing is in his blood. The way I see it, Mark set out to make me look stupid and himself look good on TV by pretending he couldn't fight and had never boxed before. That is sly – it's like stabbing a man in the back. I sat for a few days and fumed about it, going over and over it, how if I had fought properly I could have beaten him any time, and if we had a fight on my terms, I would tear him apart.

Eventually I rang him up and said, 'Right, Mark. You were bang out of order. Let's meet up and have it out. I want a proper fight with ya, not some poncy little set-up that you create just to make yourself look good.'

But he just laughed and said, 'No, I already had a fight with you! I beat you, and I don't want to do it again. Just drop it.'

And that was it. That was the last time I spoke to Mark. And good on him, he has gone on to do well, and I'll not knock it. It is good to see anyone from TOWIE do well but I will never forgive him for that fight. It took my pride away. That was the only thing we had where I grew up: our toughness. Round my way, when you had a fight you had to win or you lost all credibility. So losing that fight really knocked my self-esteem and my pride. I never regret anything, but losing that fight to Mark near on fucking killed me.

In the meantime, Sugar Hut was massively benefiting from the show. Not only was TOWIE reminding the locals that the club was up and running again, but people were now travelling from elsewhere to visit. Fans were coming to Brentwood to see what the place was like, and to try and catch a glimpse of some of the cast, because we were all in there partying a fair bit whether the cameras were rolling or not.

But on a personal level, I was suffering. My anxiety was getting worse and worse. I had never liked the idea of people talking about me or looking at me, and now they really were. Of course I always imagined the worst. If I was walking down the road and heard someone laughing, I would be sure it was at me, so I'd do one of two things. If I was feeling aggressive, I'd turn round, and say, 'What the fuck are you laughing at?' And most of the time that left the person looking shocked, because it was nothing to do with me – they'd just been laughing at something with their friends. I'd feel really bad for being so aggressive, and a bit stupid.

Or if I was feeling especially insecure, I'd have to go into the nearest shop and take my coat off to check no one had pinned something on me, and look in the mirror to make sure there was nothing daft about me they could be laughing at, like bird poo on my hair, or my jumper being inside out.

I hated going anywhere on my own. If there was someone else there at least I had a distraction, so if I wanted to go to Lakeside or shopping or whatever, I had to take someone with me. At the very least I'd have to be on the phone so that I could at least feel there was someone with me.

I imagined that everyone hated me and thought I was an idiot and was laughing at me. It sounds crazy, I know, but the fame made my insecurities a million times worse. When you are on TV, every bit of you is being scrutinized – people have a certain perception of you, and they judge you a lot more than they would otherwise.

I always made sure I kept the advice of two people in my head in those first few months of being known. The first was from Dappy. He told me, 'Remember your fans, bruv – they are the ones who can make or break you, so if someone wants to speak to you, do them the respect of giving them the time.' And I had seen him do that when we walked through clubs – if anyone wants to talk to him, he'll stop and speak to them, even if it is just a few words.

The other bit of advice – randomly – was from Chris Moyles, who I bumped into at an event. He told me, 'Kirk, fame is the best and the worst thing ever, but whatever you do, don't let it go to your head. Always stay humble. Oh, and behave yourself, because if the papers pick up on anything bad, it can totally ruin your career!'

So from day one I did my best to follow that advice, while trying to keep myself happy and sane at the same time. By the time series two was starting, Dad had decided he did want a piece of TOWIE after all. And while I was happy for him to come on board because I thought it would be fun to film with him, I was less happy for two other reasons. Firstly it meant my mum couldn't be on there any more, and while TOWIE didn't pay us for the first series, by the second series we were to be paid £50 a day. Not a lot at all, but that money would have been good for my mum, and I felt like doing the show gave her a sense of purpose, and a way to put herself out there a bit, so I was gutted. I also wanted to carry on showing the real me – Mum was, and is, a massive part of my life.

But the other reason I wasn't so happy about him coming on the show is that he wanted the world to know that Sugar Hut was his. That would have been fine if it had been clear from series one, but he had told me, 'Go on, son, you pretend you own it.' Now, though, that had changed.

I said, 'Dad, if you come barrelling in now, as the big club owner, you're gonna make me look like a right twat!' But there was no way around it, and sure enough there was a backlash and I took a fair bit of flak for it, with people thinking I was a pretender who in reality was living off my dad.

And then, right at the start of the second series, I did something I am really not proud of – I split up with Lauren on the show. It was horrible and awful, and I never want to go through anything like that again – or put anyone else through it.

This was the one thing she had always asked me not to do. Whenever we talked about our relationship away from the cameras, she would say, 'Please, Kirk, if you ever want to break up with me, don't do it on TOWIE, do it away from the cameras.'

The thing was, I had been having doubts for a few reasons. First, I was thinking that while I did love her, that spark and the lust weren't there any more. I do think that matters, but at the same time I didn't want to lose her. Yeah, I loved being near Lauren, and I wanted to touch her when she was around, but I didn't want to grab her all the time and kiss her.

But also, our lifestyles were very different. The age gap never bothered me – in fact I liked her being more mature. But her friends are so different to mine. She started modelling young and made her money early, and became mates with a lot of the London West End glamour set. I wasn't comfortable in those circles, and she couldn't come round to mine and relax with the boys I grew up with. She is a very talented career

woman – although I don't think this comes across properly on
TOWIE – and she has worked her arse off, and her hair extension
company sells products by the thousands. But it was like her
life and mine didn't fit together that well, and it was doing my
nut in. It also wasn't helped by her friend Maria, who I felt was
forever interfering in our relationship. Despite having set us up,
it felt like she was jealous of the time we spent together, and
would pick fights with me, or try and tell Lauren I wasn't treating her right. I couldn't stand her in the end, but because she
and Lauren were so close it was sometimes hard to get away
from Maria.

So with everything added together, I was thinking about
breaking up with Lauren, but wanted to respect her by doing it
off air.

The TOWIE producers would have regular meetings with us
to find out what was going on in our lives, so they could work
out what to film for the show. I found it was always better to be
honest, otherwise I might end up being filmed doing something
that wasn't me. So I said to one of them, 'I might break up with
Lauren. I'm not sure yet, but I'm not that happy. I love her, but
I don't know if I'm in love with her.'

And straight away they said, 'Great, well, this week we'll
film your break-up scene.'

'No, I can't do it on air,' I said quickly. 'The only thing Lauren
has ever asked of me is not to split up with her on TV. I understand where she's coming from, and I can't do that to her. Can't
I break up with her off-screen, then film a scene with my dad
talking about it?'

But they pointed out that the relationship was being played out in real time on the show so they couldn't have storylines happening off air – it wouldn't make sense to the viewers. And this is what I had signed up for.

And when you are in that *TOWIE* bubble, well, you don't feel you can say no. Even though I didn't like some aspects of being famous, it was my job, and I did enjoy it on some levels, so I felt I had to go with what they said.

The problem with *TOWIE* is they like to take a relationship as far as it can go, and of course the fights and the anger that come out after a break up make good TV so they want that too. They build it up, but they know that if it turns out it wasn't right, people want to see it crushed.

I thought, 'OK, I'll have to go with this. Lauren will understand because she knows how the show works, but I need to at least give her a heads-up to warn her, so she can get prepared.'

But they obviously knew I would do that, so they took my phone off me. 'Right, we're filming this scene in Sugar Hut in ten minutes. Let's get down there now!'

And, ugh, it was the worst scene I've ever had to do on *TOWIE*. Sugar Hut happened to be full of extras, all listening in. If you watch it again you will see I am crying before Lauren even turned up because I was so gutted at what I was about to have to do. And when she came I couldn't even get my words out. I could see that she knew what was happening, and was so angry and hurt. I think I just about said, 'I can't do this no more,' and she stormed out. I split up with her in public in the club and on TV, and I never wanted to do that. By signing up for *TOWIE* I signed up to put my life out there, but looking back, I feel Lauren didn't deserve that from someone who had said they loved her.

The cameras followed Lauren, not me, straight after our split and she was in the toilet crying. I was crying back out in the club and was in a total state, a real bad way. I was so upset at what I'd done, but at the same time I couldn't see any way out of it. Then I walked out and found my dad in tears at the bottom of the stairs in the club. It was the first time I had ever seen him cry.

'I never want to see you like that again,' he told me. 'I've tried my best to make sure you don't get upset in life, so it was not nice to see you like that. Just make sure you do what's right for you.'

Then, because I felt like I had broken up with Lauren before I was sure, and I missed her like crazy, after just a few days I got back together with her. I had to apologize a lot, and promise that things were going to be different. I told her that this time we should do it properly and move in together, and she was up for that. So she moved in to my house, and we found that we were really good at living together. It somehow made sense, and it was nice to have someone there to share things with, and curl up on the sofa with at night and watch a film. I set up an office in the house where she could do her work, and we'd go out for meals and just chill.

Lauren was really understanding about my life as well, and encouraged me in a lot of ways. Like eating in front of someone – I have always hated it, but it was different with her. Somehow

I felt relaxed, and like she wasn't judging me, so after a while I was happy to eat with her and not worry.

There was only one thing we disagreed about – she still wanted to go out, up in the West End, and that is not my thing. When I'm in a couple, I think, 'It's your company I like, so I just want to stay in with you, not go and hang out with a load of people I'm not bothered about.'

Then around this time we both decided to get nose jobs – she didn't like her nose, and I didn't like mine, ever since it had been broken in the fight with Mark. So we booked in to get them done – kind of like a his-and-hers operation!

It was a horrible op, though – there was a lot more pain afterwards than I had expected, and we had to stay at home for two weeks after that, while our noses recovered. And that is when things started to go wrong. We really got on top of each other. We were arguing non-stop, and I started questioning whether we really were right for each other. I was thinking, 'Right, she would make an amazing wife, and an amazing mum,' and although I was only twenty-two, I was ready for kids – but she wasn't, even though she was seven years older. And I wondered if there was any point in falling for her even harder, if we didn't want the same thing

Even once we could leave the house, I still felt that way, so I knew I had to break up with her again. I didn't know how to do it, so I texted and asked her to make sure she was in that night, as we needed to talk. I think she knew what was coming because she looked upset when I got home. I sat on the pool table in the games room and said, 'Sorry, Lauren, but I don't think it's working. You really are a great girl, but we want different things, and I can't see it ever matching up. Stay here until you find a place and I'll sleep on the sofa, but I do think we need to end things.'

She wasn't happy, and told me she thought I was wrong, but she left it at that. Lauren is a proud girl and not the type to start hysterically screaming that we need to give it another go, or whatever.

I really won't have a bad word said about Lauren. She is a total angel and such a nice girl, she never did anything wrong to me, and was never anything but amazing during our time together. It was me who wasn't always fair in our relationship. I was worried about losing her altogether, but luckily we have managed to become close friends now, which I'm so happy about. We even give each other advice on our love lives!

At the same time, during series two I was going through a different secret torment that I didn't let viewers know about. My beloved nan, mum's mum, had been getting really ill with senile dementia. She and my granddad had been living in a little house of their own since retiring from their jobs as school caretakers, and I had always kept in close contact with them. I was forever going round for my cup of tea that Nan called a 'Kirk Special' – extra strong with six spoons of sugar! We'd still bake cakes together as well – no matter how old I got I loved doing that with her. Going to see them really kept me grounded. If she was alive today I would still be over there with her. She was a star and I loved her.

At first she had started getting weird, just forgetting the time, but then she would forget who people were. So she and my granddad had moved again, this time into sheltered housing – where they were still in a private home of their own, but with support. It was in a complex with a 24-hour nurse who would keep an eye on them and bring them food if they needed it.

Nan's dementia eventually got so bad that she didn't know if it was day or night, and would keep forgetting who Granddad was. I'd go round and she would point at him and ask me, 'Who is this strange man in my house? Why is he living with me? Get him out!'

Mum was so upset by it, it really cut her up, so I tried to go and see her even more than usual to support her. I would often get her food shopping for her anyway, but at this time I was trying to do more than that, to make sure she had as little as possible to worry about.

It must have been so terrible for Granddad. The woman he loved, who he had been with for 50 years, didn't even know who he was. She even tried to climb out of the window once to escape when she saw him and got frightened. Eventually they had to put her in a care home, and she was looked after there. And although she was still alive, I think for Granddad in a way she had already died. Her spirit had kind of faded and disappeared.

He said to my mum, 'Julie, I can't really do this without Jean. Life seems pretty pointless without her.' And he stopped eating. It was like my other grandparents. Their marriage had been proper old school, where they were each other's worlds. It is the kind of marriage I want to have. They were still making each other laugh after years and years together, and they would still be holding hands as they walked down the street. I want to fall in love on that level, where I look at someone and think, 'I want to grow old with you. I want to marry you not to prove to other people how in love we are, but to prove it to ourselves.'

No one today seems to fall in love like that, where they physically die without the other person, but that is what happened to Granddad. He just faded away; he weighed only four and a half stone when he died in hospital in March 2011.

I couldn't go into the hospital towards the end because he looked so ill and tiny, and I couldn't bear to see it. He was a great, happy guy, and that is the memory I hold on to.

Sadly, shortly after this my Uncle Dennis, my mum's sister Terry's husband, became ill with cancer. He was a great guy who loved me and Daniel and always looked out for us growing up. But he was in hospital for months and it was very upsetting, but I couldn't face seeing him. I had had enough of hospitals and sickness. Instead I would pray for him. The religious beliefs that had been instilled in me at my Catholic school, and during weekly trips to church, were and still are strong in me, and I thought praying for my uncle was the right thing to do. I'm not sure if things like that do work, but thinking positive thoughts about someone and praying that they will get better can only be a good thing.

Besides, I like to think Jesus was a pretty good dude, and that he might help me out if he can! So I would still happily go to church now, even if it meant going on my own. I have no problem doing that. I still question the walking on water thing, though. My theory is he was just an early ice skater . . .

Anyway, I was the only one in the family who hadn't been to see my uncle in hospital, and in the end Aunty Terry said to me, 'Please go and see him. He wants to see you!'

'What do I say?'

'Talk about anything, he just wants to hear your voice.'

So in the end I did go to the hospital, and it was horrible to see my uncle lying there. I just about managed to say, 'Hi, Uncle Del, it's Kirk here, I hope you are OK.' But I wasn't sure if he could hear me.

I went to Sugar Hut later that night with my cousin Scott, and at one point he got a call to tell him that Uncle Del had died. His mum – my aunt Tina – told Scott he had been holding out to see me, and then he relaxed afterwards and died happy. But it just added to my hatred of hospitals. I felt like I must have jinxed him by going in, and so I vowed that I would never go in a hospital again.

Over that summer I did a lot of PAs – public appearances – and interviews. I had taken on management outside of the show to organize this for me, as most of the cast now did. The show didn't pay that well so this is how we earned the real money.

My interviews were mainly with the weekly celebrity magazines, like Star, New!, Now and Reveal. I would talk openly about the latest happenings on the show and my thoughts on whatever relationship I was in at the time. Mostly there would be a photoshoot to go alongside it. I think my favourite shoot was for *Star* magazine, where they had me stripped to my boxers in the middle of a laundrette in Wapping, like something out of the old Levi's jeans advert starring Nick Kamen. There were dozens of local kids crowded at the window looking in, and I didn't know whether to be chuffed to bits or mortified! It was good fun, though, and the pictures were great.

I also did a few interviews with the gay media, like *Attitude* magazine and *Gay Times*, as well as some shoots, including one where I was completely naked while a load of guys threw buckets of water over me. Surreal! I always take it as a massive compliment to be asked as a straight guy to be on the cover of a gay mag.

I do have this mad big gay following, and I love it! I have always been popular with gay lads, even growing up I think it is because I'm quite pretty, if you know what I mean – I have quite feminine features, but at the same time I'm a bit of a rugged-looking boy. Gay fans are really loyal, and tweet me loads – it is great to have them. I love lesbian fans too, though – and I have plenty of their merchandise as well, ha!

Doing PAs basically means being paid to appear at a venue, so they mainly involve going to nightclubs, but also bars, shopping centres, wherever. They are easy money on one level – generally about £3,000 per appearance – and mostly I would be expected to go on stage or into the DJ booth and say a few words for a couple of minutes, just to get the crowd a bit hyped up. Then maybe I would do a signing and some photos, and then just chill at a table and enjoy free drinks for the rest of the night. In a good weekend I could be earning £12k. Not bad!

I used some of the money to get Mum's house redecorated for her as a present. She had moved around a few times, and never lived anywhere very nice, but she seemed happier with her house at that time, so I decided that if she was going to stay there, I would do my best to make it as nice as possible. That was a really good feeling. Until then I had been able to give her money and presents, but this was the first really big difference I was able to make in her life. I know, though, that it was only a small way of repaying everything she did for me when I was growing up, and I still have a long way to go.

But although the money was good, I started to hate doing the PAs. They brought out my anxiety in a big way and I started to suffer bad panic attacks. I can't remember the first time it happened, but every time I would go to a PA, I would start to worry on the way. 'Why am I doing this? Who do I think I am that people are going to come to a club to see me? Everyone will be looking at me, thinking, "Who the fuck is this geezer? What a twat," and they'll hate me.'

I'd get more and more worked up until I was just about to go on stage, then the first sign of a panic attack would kick in – my fingers start to tingle. They start to go numb, and then I breathe in and it feels like it is the last breath I will ever take, so I panic more. Then my breath will get shorter and shorter and I feel like I am going to faint, bang right there on the floor.

A panic attack is like a build-up of adrenalin, a load of energy that you can't release. I didn't know this at the time, and couldn't understand what was happening to me. But I didn't want to talk to anyone about it, so I tried to deal with it myself and work out my own solutions. The best way to get past that panic is to release the adrenalin somehow. I didn't realize that is what I was doing, and it sounds weird, but I found that shouting was the best way to get the adrenalin out. If I could, I used to try to shout and be active before I got on stage, or even have an argument. I also started working with two tour managers, Ian Stoddart and Dave Almond from Peace of Mind, who would make sure I got to the PA on time, take care of my security, and so on. It was reassuring to have them around, as they would take the edge off my nerves a bit. They didn't even have to say anything – they could tell what was going on in my mind, and would do everything to make sure I got a bit of space.

Then once on stage I would shake my hands to get my circulation going, and dance around to keep using up the energy. It sounds ridiculous, but at least to everyone watching it would look like I was having a good time!

It got so bad that I was doing anything to get out of attending the PAs. Despite the nice pay cheque at the end, I hated them, and I felt that the money didn't make up for the mental torture I was putting myself through to be there.

Amy left TOWIE at the end of the second series. I think she hadn't had as much air time during that series as the first, and she was annoyed. She also thought she could go off and do her own thing, and be bigger than TOWIE. So she went into the Celebrity Big Brother house in September 2011.

197

I am a massive fan of the show, so of course I was going to watch if there was someone I knew on it. Amy and I still hadn't really talked since series one, when I thought she had made me look like an idiot to boost her own image, but I wanted to see how she would get on. And I thought she did well.

I texted her when she came out to say well done, and we fell into general talking. We didn't dwell on the past – I don't like to go over old arguments, I just prefer to be like, 'How ya doing?' and start from scratch. And we did that, and got to being mates again – and this time only mates!

Instead my head was completely taken over by another girl – Gemma Massey. Ahh, Gemma, the most perfect girl I have ever met, apart from one massive problem: she was a porn star.

Not that it was a problem in the beginning. In fact, that was what made me want to meet her. She was friends with my mate, so I said, 'Introduce me! I wanna shag a porn star! Wahey, that'll be good!'

I know that sounds bad, but come on – it must be every lad's dream. So we met up, and we got on, and she ended up back at my flat, and we had sex, and, yes, it was as amazing as I had imagined. We seemed to fit together physically on every level. The next morning we woke up next to each other and I was just lying in bed looking at her, thinking, 'Wow, you are perfect.'

She had beautiful long dark hair, an amazing figure, really smooth, tanned skin, and what I always like in a girl – great fake boobs and pouty lips. But I loved her personality too. She had lots to say and was really down to earth and fun. We really clicked, and had such a laugh together, talking for hours on end. I fell in love with her then and there.

Even though it wasn't what I had planned, it was like a relationship began over the next few days. I found that I was really developing feelings for her, so I stopped for a moment and thought about it. I said to myself, 'I can't do this, she is a porn star! Am I supposed to date someone who spends her days having sex with other people? There's no way I can cope with that!'

But rather than just tell her that, and attempt to explain what I was feeling, I tried to convince myself she was a bad person, to make it easier to cut her off. So I was horrible to her, even though I loved her to pieces, and accused her of all sorts of things, even though the poor girl didn't deserve it. I made her cry, and sure enough she left, which is what I had wanted. It was really wrong of me to do that to her, but I just couldn't be the person to leave, as I had liked her so much. The way I behaved is something I feel bad about to this day.

TWELVE

Celebrity Big Brother

Meantime in September 2011 I had taken on new management. At the launch party for the website for Sam and Billie Faiers' shop, Minnie's, which we held in Sugar Hut, I started talking to Sam's manager, Adam Muddle, who had previously also managed Brian Belo, and we decided to work together. I liked what he had done with Sam, and he had some good ideas for me that didn't just involve doing as many PAs as possible to make some quick cash, and so I started to get quite excited about the future.

Before we could put any of this into practice, series three of *TOWIE* started, and, well, straight away I wasn't enjoying it. The one bit I did like was my bromance with Joey Essex. He had joined the show in series two, and now that I was single we had a proper good laugh. Joey was like a little brother to me, and I wanted to look out for him. He was good fun as well, and we would go out together doing stupid things. We combined our names to take the piss out of all the famous duos who did that, and called ourselves Team Jirk!

But Joey was really the only good thing for me in that series. Dad had started dating Maria Fowler, and I wasn't a fan of hers. She had interfered too much in my relationship with Lauren, and caused a lot of problems there. And I hated the idea that she was hanging off my dad's arm just to get some more air time on the show. The relationship didn't last long after a national newspaper ran a story about claims Maria had worked as an escort (something she has denied) but the whole thing still left me with a bad feeling.

Also I didn't get on well with the producers at the time, and I felt like they were only ever showing me in a bad light. Every single scene had me asking Dad for money, or arguing. The money thing wasn't fair, because the agreement with my dad had always been that I would get a basic salary at Sugar Hut, but it would be topped up with bonuses, as I was doing so well for the club. So I would get £300 a week as my staff payment, which is lower than what I should have been getting, and then Dad would do something like buy me a car, which would more than make up for my low salary. But the way it was shown on TOWIE, I was just the scrounging son asking for yet another thing off my dad, and doing no work for it, and it was frustrating. People were abusing me on Twitter, thinking I was this spoilt brat who had been brought up with money, and didn't know anything about a hard life, which was completely wrong.

The producers also liked to show me getting fiery in arguments, particularly with girls. In everyday life I hardly ever argue with girls – in fact, I love women! But I had argued a lot with Maria during the second series, and it spilled over into the third. The thing was, as I watched the shows back I felt like I was starting to learn something about myself and my anger. While I had always thought it was all down to simply having a bad temper that I struggled to control, combined with the ADHD when I was younger, I now started to think there might be more to it. Every time I lost my temper on screen, it followed directly from a situation where I was on edge and anxious about something – a moment when I thought everyone was judging me, or making a fool out of me, and my anxiety was kicking in. And I started to think, 'Is my anger a part of that? Am I lashing out because my adrenalin is so crazy high that I don't know how else to get rid of it, and that is how it comes out?'

It was a different way of looking at it, and I was now realizing for the first time exactly what anxiety is, and in how many different ways it can show itself. I began to do a bit of research into it, which didn't really make me any more in control, but at least I felt I better understood my temper after that.

Meanwhile, I was sick of being called things like 'wife-beater' on Twitter because Maria was playing the sympathy card – I've never hit a woman in my life! I just thought, 'I don't need this. My being on TOWIE has done what I needed it to do in terms of helping Sugar Hut, and I'm happy with my job there, so I'm going to go back to that.' There was a lot more to me than what they were showing, but it felt as if the storylines were putting me in a bad light, so I was out of there.

When I left, I had no intention of doing anything more on TV. I didn't like the life it was giving me then, and I didn't need it.

People thought I was trying to do a Mark Wright, as he was leaving at the same time to try and get into TV presenting, but I wasn't after that at all. I felt like I was struggling to work myself out. I'd found that all the problems in my head were only exaggerated by fame, so I wanted to step away from the limelight and get myself back on track.

Despite everything that had been going on during series three of TOWIE, there was one person I couldn't get out of my head: Gemma. We hadn't talked since she had left a couple of months before, but I thought about her every single day. I felt sick that I wasn't with her, and when I woke up each morning she was on my mind. Everything reminded me of Gemma; every love song I heard would instantly take my mind back to her. It was driving me crazy, and just when I thought things should have been getting easier, and I should have been getting over her, my feelings were only growing stronger.

Eventually I caved in. She was in America, but I called her up and said, 'Gemma, I know you don't want to talk to me, but I wanted to say I don't care if you are a porn star. I miss you too much, and I want you back. I can't not be with you.' It was so good to talk to her again.

'If you're big enough to say that,' she told me, 'I want to be with you too. I'll quit my job for you. I just have two more commitments, then that's it – I'll give up porn.'

It was the dream response. She still wanted to be with me, and she was giving up her job without me asking! I thought this was it – this was my future wife. When she hung up I called the hotel she was in and said, 'Please send the biggest and best bouquet of flowers you have up to Gemma Massey's room, and tell her I love her!'

From the minute she was back in the UK, we became proper close. And I mean proper close. We were together all the time, and just the feeling of being around her was incredible. I couldn't stop touching her or wanting to be with her. If she left the house just to go down to the shops, I missed her.

It drove me crazy when she went off to do the two scenes for the porn movie she was still on contract to do. The idea that she was going to have sex with this other guy when she was my girlfriend killed me! But it was the same guy in both scenes, and I told myself she was doing nothing wrong. This was her job before I met her, and she was giving it up for me – we just had to get through those two days. And it was difficult, but we did it.

While it was just the two of us in our relationship, working everything through and having opinions on how we should do things, it was great. But the problem was that I was famous, so the two of us couldn't be alone for long.

One of our dates was at Winter Wonderland, a Christmas market and ice rink that gets set up in Hyde Park every year. We went in November and had such good fun there, and got papped messing around on the ice. You can see in the pictures how happy I look with Gemma, but once it was out there that I was dating a porn star, the Twitter abuse started.

I have always had a love/hate relationship with Twitter. I really like being able to chat with fans and friends on it, and to see what is happening in everyone else's lives. But there are so many idiots who just use it to throw abuse. Half of the time they don't even know or mean what they are saying, they just want a reaction, but you know my personality – I find it really hard not to react! And dating Gemma was like handing all the little trolls a load of ammunition.

I was constantly getting messages calling her a slag, or pictures of her in porn films having sex with another guy, while the tweeter told me what they had enjoyed watching her do. I tried to ignore it, but I couldn't; it played with my head, and we would row about it. I really took it out on Gemma and it wasn't her fault. It was like I had fallen in love with the wrong person, and I couldn't decide whether or not I could handle everything that came with her.

When we were hidden away in my house, in our own little world, I felt like there was nothing I couldn't face if I was with her. Then the next day I'd see an especially nasty tweet and it would get my mind working. Even though I was madly in love with her, and I could handle it for now, how would I deal with it in the future? If we got married I would want to be the only one who sees my girl naked, the only one having sex with her and knowing what it is like, rather than half the UK male population being able to watch her in action somewhere online. Take it a step further. Say we had kids and they were at school. Even if Gemma hadn't done porn for years, the Internet makes it impossible to hide this sort of thing away. One day one of the kids might pull my kid over to a computer and say, 'Look at this, here is your mum getting fucked by another guy.' How the hell am I supposed to decide that is what I want for our future? Then

I'd go and spend a day on my own with Gemma again, and know that I loved her so much it didn't matter.

My head was all over the place. And it didn't help that everyone else had an opinion, especially when it came to my image. My dad really liked Gemma, but kept telling me, 'Kirk, you can't be with her. I get that she is a really lovely girl, but it doesn't make you look good.'

And my manager, Adam, would tell me, 'She's lovely, but you need to decide what you want from your future, because if you want any TV work, you can't stay with her.'

So Gemma and I would row and break up for a day, but I would feel shit straight away, and I know she did too, and so one of us would text or call the other. Then we would get back together, and it was on and off, but I was getting pissed off with everyone else, and I kept telling them I didn't want to be famous. I had left *TOWIE* for a reason, and I just wanted to get on with a normal existence. I couldn't help that I loved Gemma, and I wanted everyone to stop tormenting me, and just let me be with her.

And I did that. I kept trying to step away from 'celebland', but it's not so easy once you have stepped in. Then *Celebrity Big Brother* got in touch. Now, I have been a huge fan of that show since day one – you might almost say obsessive. You know those people who would sit up watching the live feed when it used to run through the night? Watching the housemates sleeping and going, 'Oh quick, look at him, he's rolling over!', then five minutes later, 'Listen to that, is she snoring? How funny!'? Yep, pathetic I know, but I loved it!

So to be asked to go on . . . well, there was no way I could say no, so all my plans to turn down any television work went out the window. Oh, and did I mention they offered me a lot of money to do it? If I needed a little nudge (although I didn't) that would have been it.

My first thought was to get in shape. I've never had a bad body, but knowing I'd be filmed in the shower, bed, getting changed . . . I wanted to be in the best shape of my life! My friend Kenzie – a rapper from Blazin' Squad who had been in the CBB house himself for series three – was now working as a personal trainer, so I got his services in. He had me working out non-stop – on the weights in the gym, running round the park, all sorts of circuits. You name it, we did it!

Meantime I was still with Gemma – in fact, we were tighter than ever. No matter what people had said to me about her, I knew she was right for me and I wanted to stick with her. We spent Christmas and New Year together, and I even got her to join in with my baking obsession, and we made gingerbread men on Christmas Eve! She made her one to look like me, and I made one that looked like her. They were really cute, and it was a great evening.

Then on New Year's Eve we stayed at the May Fair hotel in London and watched the fireworks from our balcony. It was a really homely, romantic, coupley time, where I could see what a future with Gemma could be like, and I liked what I saw.

But I assumed that one of the reasons the *Celebrity Big Brother* producers had wanted me is because I have the image of being a ladies' man, and I wouldn't be very popular with them if I went into the house in a relationship. I told Gemma my concerns and we talked about whether I should pretend I was single and still stay with her, but that seemed daft. Gemma was upset, but she said, 'I think you need to put your career first. So let's just split up, and you go in the house, and if we feel the same in a few weeks when you are out again, we can always pick things up from where we left off.' I thought she was right. I really wanted to do *Celebrity Big Brother*, and I knew if we were a strong enough couple then a few weeks apart wouldn't matter, so we ended it.

In January 2012 I went into the *Big Brother* house, which is built at the back of Elstree Studios in west London. People have since asked if I was worried about panic attacks and anxiety before I went in, but I wasn't. The excitement of it all overrode any other feelings. And wow, what an experience it turned out to be!

I was totally amazed when I went in the house to see Michael Madsen there. That man is one of my idols. In *Reservoir Dogs* he blows me away. Here was an actor from one of my favourite films of all time, standing right in front of me. And I was getting to live with him!

Going in is a strange experience because you think, 'That's it.' You forget your life in the outside world, and all the contestants get on like they are at home and are going to live in there for ever. People were taking their tops off and wandering around, getting in the hot tub and swimming, opening up about their deepest secrets . . . I loved it!

I had a great bunch of housemates in with me, and I really

got caught up in it all, so much so that I didn't think of Gemma. Not in a bad way, like I didn't care about her, but my mind was overwhelmed with everything else.

You soon realize how boring it can be, though. There is nothing to do. So you start making everything take twice as long as it needs to. You will wake up and lie in bed relaxing. Then get up and make breakfast really slowly, and eat it, enjoying every mouthful. Then you will have a shower, and make that the longest, hottest shower possible. And by the time you get out and get changed, you hope it is time for lunch! That is how ridiculous it is.

Frankie Cocozza quickly became my best mate. He had been on the last series of X Factor and I had met him down at the studios, and we had been BBMing since then. But it was only in the house that we got to be really tight. I thought he was the bollocks, and I loved that he really didn't give a fuck. He thought, said and did what he wanted, and I admired that about him.

In a way my friendship with him made me come a bit unstuck as far as the show went, though, as it fitted even more with the role they wanted me to take on. Everyone in the Big Brother house starts to fall into a role for the producers – a bit like in TOWIE – but this time I was cast in the role of a womanizing bad boy. I can't pretend I didn't deserve it on one level, but it was not what I was about. I cooked all the time and was the obsessive cleaner in the house. I cleaned that place every day, literally got down on my hands and knees and scrubbed the bathroom floor with bleach – you had to with that many people living there, or it would have been vile! I taught the others how to wash their clothes in the bath and survive without a washing machine. And they didn't show any of that on air!

But I can see where the womanizing thing came from. Basically I was flirting with Irish model Georgia Salpa. She was a good-looking girl, and I did fancy her looks – although not her personality. I never felt like she had much to say. I didn't actually want to date her, but there was nothing else to do, so flirting with her passed the time. Then one night after we had been in there for a week, Natasha Giggs, who I got on well with as a mate, asked me to get into bed with her, not to do anything, just for a cuddle – but the minute I put my foot in I thought of Gemma and was overwhelmed with guilt. I ran to the diary room and cried my eyes out about her. I said, 'Listen, I split up with the girl I love to do this game show, this is not right!'

And from then on it was like that had opened the floodgates. It brought back the reality of the outside world, and burst the bubble I had been living in. I couldn't stop talking about Gemma and my life back home in general. I'd be in the diary room crying my eyes out, saying how much I missed her and missed home. I am a proper crier when I get going! But mix that with me flirting with Georgia . . . and, well, I get why once it had been edited to cut out all the hours in between, I looked like a bit of a playboy.

Editing is a funny thing. When I came out of the house and heard what the public thought of certain people, I'd wonder, how the hell did they get that idea? Everyone seemed to think Denise Welch was a raging fruit loop, always on the drink. But we had two bottles of wine and twenty beers to share between the whole house every night, so how could someone be a piss-head on that? In reality Denise was lovely. All she ever talked about were her kids. She was one of my favourites in that house, along with Natasha, Nicola McLean, Natalie Cassidy and Gareth Thomas. They were all so lovely!

One moment on the show that I wasn't so happy about was my geography task . . . I was pulled into the diary room and asked to mark out certain places on a map. I had told them before I went in that I would hate to do anything that involved general knowledge, or something you learned in school, so they obviously thought it would be funny to give me that! And it was bad. I couldn't even tell where America was on the map. I haven't got a clue on that stuff, because I didn't take it in at school. I figured I would never actually need it anyway. But that day was really embarrassing.

It was so emotional in that house, but despite everything, and the editing and whatever else, it was still one of the best things I ever did in my life. It was like I had ticked a teenage dream off the list!

When I left the house after sixteen days – I was the fourth person to be evicted – I didn't know what I was going to come out to. I was still madly in love with Gemma and wanted to make things right with her, and I had no idea what reaction I would get from the public. It is a weird feeling, not knowing how you will be perceived. And actually I got a lot of cheers so I was happy with that. I remember I even asked at the time, 'Was the number to vote for me not working right? 'Cos that response was so positive!'

There were suggestions that because it was a vote to save the housemates for once, rather than the usual vote to evict, viewers had got confused, and voted for the wrong people. But that is only speculation; I will never know and I just had to accept it.

I had my exit interview live with Brian Dowling and he asked me, 'Who do you want to actually be with, Georgia or Gemma?'

And straight away I said, 'Gemma! I came in here single and the girl I split up with – I regret every minute of it – and I have just realized how much I love her and I really do.'

I had no idea if she was watching, and whether she hated me or still wanted to be with me. I called her as soon as I could, and it turned out she had gone off to Dubai while the show was on to escape the press, as they had all been asking her for interviews while I was in the house. When I had been doing my interview with Brian, Gemma's mum had called her out there on Skype, and had the laptop turned to face the TV, so she saw what I had said about her.

As soon as I got through to her I said, 'Sorry, I have been such an idiot.'

'I heard what you said,' she told me. 'Did you mean it?'

'Yeah, I love you!'

'Well, I'm getting on the next flight home to you then,' she said.

And I was so pleased that she was doing that. I couldn't wait to see her again. But I still had work to do, so I headed back to the hotel where they put me up so I could talk to the press about the whole *Celebrity Big Brother* experience.

But then Natasha came over to the hotel. She had been evicted before me, so she came to see me and catch up. Natasha had become famous for having an eight-year affair with Ryan Giggs – the brother of her husband, Rhodri. She and Rhodri were separated by then. The two of us had got on in the house, but just as friends – we had never even flirted, but I did really like her. And, well, things just happened that night.

That sounds bad, doesn't it, when Gemma was on her way back from Dubai to see me. But my head was all over the place. Natasha was an attractive girl, even though I hadn't allowed myself to think it in the house. Combine that with the fact I felt pretty confused and alone when I got out of the house, and it was like I had a connection with her as the only one who really understood what I was thinking at that time. She had been in the house, really seen what was going on and what it was like, and was feeling similar emotions to me.

But the next day, as I was getting back to Essex, so was Gemma. She had literally run to the airport the night before and got on the first plane home. It was really romantic, like something out of a film! But we couldn't be seen, so Adam had arranged for a car to take Gemma to a nearby hotel and I met her there, so we could catch up without any paps getting pictures of us. I needed to get my head straight without anyone else giving their opinions or judgement.

We had a great first night back together, and it was so good to see her, but almost immediately reality kicked in. Although I was off Celebrity Big Brother, the many interviews and appearances we were expected to do afterwards were about to start.

I told Adam, 'Gemma is back, she's my girlfriend, and I want people to know that, no matter what.'

But he told me, 'To be honest, mate, you've got a lot of work to do in the next few weeks. You need to focus on that, not on a girl, and especially not one where you're going to be linked to all the porn stuff.'

So again, poor Gemma was great – she understood, and she said, 'You gotta do what you gotta do. Let's leave things for weeks, months, whatever it takes.' And she left and got on with her own life. And somehow, although I would have loved it to, my relationship with her never really started up again. She didn't trust me to stick it out with her again, and not give her grief over her old life or go running off when something came up for work. And I get that. I understand how she felt, but the attraction didn't disappear. And we would occasionally meet every few months, when we were both single and in the same town, but she would never agree to actually start dating me again. Which is a shame, because I truly believe she is the one girl in my life who has been best for me, and who I have loved the most.

As soon as Gemma and I split . . . well, another thing happened. On the final night of Celebrity Big Brother, there was a wrap party for all the housemates and crew. It was really good to see everyone again and have a catch up. At one point the two Playboy twins, Kristina and Karissa Shannon, who had been in the house, came over to me and tried to chat. I had got on with them when we were first in the house, but they had talked badly

214

about me and Frankie behind our backs, and I had seen that once I was out of the house and watching the footage. So I said to them, 'You were bang out of order to me and Frankie in the house. I've watched you since leaving the house, don't forget, and I saw how much you were mugging me right off in the diary room. Do one!'

But they said, 'OK, Kirk, we're really sorry, we were only doing what we were told by our manager. He said it would make us popular in the UK if we took you and Frankie apart.'

I just shrugged it off, but later, back at the hotel, Kristina came over and told me she really fancied me. I just said, 'Are you serious? After everything in the house?!'

She got her phone out and started showing me naked pictures of herself, saying, 'Come to my room and I'll show you how much I fancy you.'

I was thinking, 'This is the last thing I was expecting, but she's a sexy girl – I'm hardly going to say no!' So, well, I didn't, and I went back to her room.

Once *Celebrity Big Brother* was over, Frankie moved into my house. He had no money, because although he had been on *X Factor*, he didn't earn anything straight away from that. But he wasn't thinking about it – he was still like a little kid when it came to his fame and everything surrounding it. When we were in the *Big Brother* house he would say, 'I can't wait to get out of the house, bro, so we can go clubbing here, holidaying there, partying here, shagging birds there ...'

But I had taken on a bit of an older brother role with him,

and I wanted to see him come good. So I said, 'Look, mate, you'll come out of here with no money, so you need to work and earn some, or you'll end up poor, fucked up and in rehab. Come and live with me for a bit, 'cos you'll get picked up easier from there for jobs like PAs and that.' He'd definitely have less trouble travelling to PAs round the country if he was in Essex, rather than in Brighton, where he was originally from.

Frankie lived with me for a month or so, and we blitzed the PAs for a bit, and we did have a proper laugh together. I still hated doing PAs, but it was easier with Frankie there – people were looking at two of you, not one. It felt like I had no choice but to do them anyway, as it was all part of my *Celebrity Big Brother* work.

I was still seeing Natasha from time to time. It wasn't a one-night thing, but it wasn't a proper relationship either. Then again if I say it was a fling, that makes it sound like it wasn't important to me, and it was. She is a really nice girl, and in a different situation, things might have worked out. But she was in the middle of trying to sort out her marriage problems and she needed some space for that.

Writing this I realize how it seems like I go between girl-friends quick, and I can't deny it, because I do. But I never cheat, I just don't really have a gap in between. I don't like being single. Not just because I love sex, but also because I love being in the company of girls. I don't know if it was growing up with my mum, so that's what I'm comfortable with, but I always like there to be a girl in my life. I feel really empty without one. Not that I get with any girl for the sake of it – at least I didn't once I was out of my teens. They all mean something to me.

Anyway, the work from *Celebrity Big Brother* died down really quickly. The hype from the show doesn't last long – everyone comes out of that house thinking they are set up for life, but it always fades away. And it didn't help that my reputation wasn't particularly good. I wasn't getting the love from the female fans any more, as they saw me as a player, and it took me ages to move away from that image once the damage was done. I still hated doing PAs, which didn't help, and then I did a couple with Frankie that didn't go too well. On the way to one of them he drank two bottles of Jack Daniel's and was a right mess by the time we arrived. He had started to annoy me a bit, and so he moved out in the end, as we were getting on top of each other too much.

THIRTEEN

Looking for Love

Throughout all of this, Amy and I were still texting, and in spring 2012 she invited me round to her house. As we were chatting like old times we found ourselves getting close again. The attraction was still there, as strong as ever, and before we knew it, things started happening, and then we were dating again. It was the same pull of old – I couldn't keep away from her! But now, for the first time, it seemed like both of us were really ready to get into a real relationship. It felt like she had grown up a bit, and as far as I knew we were both behaving ourselves with other people. We were together all the time, just getting closer and closer.

There was only one problem. By then Amy was managed by CAN Associates, run by a woman called Claire Powell, who told Amy that we had to keep our relationship secret. She wouldn't let her go out in public with me, and said it wasn't that they didn't approve of me, but it was too soon after Amy's last boyfriend – Joe, the guy she had been dating at the same time as me on TOWIE, and then had openly been with – for her to be seen out with me.

I understood why they were doing it – it doesn't look good to go from one relationship straight to another. But on the other hand, it was making things hard for us. We had to sneak around to see each other, and could hardly ever leave the house.

At the same time, because everyone else thought I was single, I was approached about doing The Bachelor for Channel 5. The show follows one single guy as he meets and dates 25 single girls, slowly cutting them down each week until he finds 'the one'. Gavin Henson had done the first show the year before and it had been really good for his profile, so I was keen to do it, and knew I would get a lot of work off the back of it. Conversations had been going back and forth on it for several months, but at the same time I didn't want to mess things up with Amy when this was the closest our relationship had ever come to working out.

So I sat down with her and said, 'Amy, I've been asked to do The Bachelor. What do you reckon?'

'No way!' She was instantly against it.

'Well, are we going to get serious? I don't want to turn it down if we're only going to split up next week.'

But she promised me, 'No, don't do it, let's give things a really good go with us and get properly serious.'

So I turned down the show, but Claire still didn't want us to go out in public, and it was causing arguments as I was getting paranoid that Amy didn't want to be seen with me. Then finally I said to her manager, 'Claire, this is making our relationship bad now. Can we do a quick press release and tell people we're together?'

'I'll tell you what, Kirk,' she said. 'It's her birthday soon. How about we wait until then? That night you can go out to her party holding hands, and everyone will see it and know that you two are dating again. I also suggest you leave your management and come to work with me, as that will make more sense when you two are openly together.'

And I thought, 'Yeah, brilliant,' and did what she advised. I felt secure about things and just got on with enjoying my time with Amy.

We were always telling each other we loved each other, and I would buy Amy presents all the time. She loves handbags, so I would buy her designer ones whenever I could. I was really falling for her and it was like she had grown up a bit, and was behaving more like we were in an adult relationship. The power struggle wasn't there as much between us, and it was like Amy was more honest with me about her feelings. She was always telling me how happy she was, and that she could see herself settling down with me. Life was perfect, and I thought to myself, 'I really could marry this girl. I think if she was my wife, we really could be happy for all our lives.'

I could see us having a family together. I'd always wanted to settle down young and be a young dad, so I could play with my own children and still relate to them as they grew up, and then one day I could go to my grandkids' weddings. Other than Gemma, Amy was the only person I had ever felt strongly enough about to see it as an option. Maybe I was getting ahead of myself but this is how I felt and I convinced myself Amy thought the same.

But then two things happened that caused horrible rows between us. The first was when it came out that she and Frankie, who she had met through me, had been sending flirty texts. Nothing had happened, but it was more the principle. I know Amy is a bit of a flirt, but I was actually more pissed off with Frankie than her over that, as I really thought he would have had my back and respected me enough not to go near her.

Then a few weeks later, Amy went off to Liverpool to film for *Celebrity Wedding Planner*. The idea was that she and Harry Derbidge were to help someone plan their wedding and it would be filmed for Channel 5. We were good at allowing each other to get on with work, as both of us would quite often be away, so I just left her to it. But then the next day I looked at the *Daily Mail* online, catching up with the news. And there were pictures of Amy coming out of a hotel with this guy, and lots of details in the story about him and what they had done the night before. It said he was David Peters, who had been on *Take Me Out*, and she had spent the night in a hotel room with him drinking wine. My girlfriend, who was supposed to tell the world we were together at a birthday in just two weeks' time, had been spending time with this guy.

I started shaking as I read it. I was so upset, and so angry. I called her up straight away and said, 'Are you fucking serious, Amy? What the fuck are you doing?'

'I'm so sorry, Kirk, but it ain't like that. Nothing happened

– we were in the bar, Harry was there too, and the papers have got it all wrong!'

'Bollocks,' I said. 'You're a fucking idiot.'

And I hung up and refused to take her calls for the next few days, even though she was leaving me all sorts of messages, apologizing and asking me to forgive her, and saying she had done nothing wrong. At the time, deep down, I was sure something had happened with this David, and I felt like she had made a fool of me and broken my heart.

She had to go to Glasgow for an event called the Fake Bake Glitz and Glamour Ball, but she kept ringing and ringing, and I kept ignoring it. Then Claire called me. She said, 'Kirk, I have never seen Amy like this. We're at the airport and are supposed to be going to Scotland, but Amy won't get on the plane unless you say you'll get back with her.'

And that made me think that she really was telling the truth – maybe she had just randomly bumped into him and had a few quick drinks, and actually I should trust her. Besides, I missed her like crazy, and I wanted her back in my life!

So I called Amy and said, 'OK, let's get back together. I'll take your word for it, just don't ever get pictured like this again in future, 'cos you made me look stupid.'

Everything seemed right again for a couple of weeks. I was looking forward to letting the world know we were a couple so we could start actually being seen out together, so the day before her birthday I went round as usual, and asked her, 'What do you want to do tomorrow? I take it the party Claire talked about isn't happening anymore as you haven't mentioned it?'

'No, I don't feel like that, I'm just going to stay in with my family.'

'OK, if that's what you feel like. It's your birthday!' I said, thinking she meant I should come over and join them for dinner or whatever. 'What time shall I come round?'

'No, I just want to do the family thing on my own, babe,' she said, not looking me in the eye.

'Well, I still want to see you. It's your birthday, and I need to give you your pressies and say happy birthday – and give ya a birthday kiss! So can I come over at some point?'

'Maybe not on my actual birthday,' she said.

So I left that day thinking there was something weird going on. She would normally be really keen for me to be there. But I hoped it was something else unrelated to me, and pushed ahead with my plans.

For her birthday, which is on 7 June, I had bought her two bags – a Mulberry one, and a Chloé one, as she loves her designer handbag collection – and I had gone to the florist and given him £1k as well, to have bouquets turning up at her house all day long. It might sound daft, but I thought it was a romantic gesture! And I decided to pop by in the morning regardless, just to drop off her pressies and say happy birthday. Her dad answered the door and said, 'Oh, Amy's in the shower. It's probably not worth you waiting, but I'll pass on the presents – thank you.'

This was weird, as normally they wouldn't think twice about inviting me in. So I gave the bags to her dad, and said, 'Tell her to call me.'

I was getting worried. There was definitely something going

on. And I found out what it was about a minute later. As I got back into my car I got a text from her that said she didn't want us to be together any more.

I sat there and cried my fucking heart out. For the first time Amy and I had really made a go of it, had both put our all into it without involving other people, and I had thought it was going to work. I'm not exaggerating when I say at that moment she broke my heart.

I was also confused as it seemed like everything had been going well. She had got me to turn down a TV show, told me she loved me, and yet suddenly she was breaking up with me. I wondered whether I should fight to get her back, but I thought, 'No, it's her call, I'm not going to make a fool of myself. She can work things through in her own mind in her own time.' I went home and just lay in bed, curled up and crying for the rest of the day.

The next day I went on *Daily Mail* online, and once again got the shock of my life. There were pictures of David Peters walking up to her house on her birthday, carrying Victoria's Secret bags. Suddenly it seemed to make sense. She had blown me out because she had invited him around, and there really had been something happening with them. That must be it.

I became obsessed with it, and started investigating. When I went back through David's tweets I saw that he had been in Vegas the week before. As far as I knew, Victoria's Secret were mostly sold in the US, so he had clearly bought her presents then, hadn't he? He must have known her measurements to buy stuff for her, and he knew it was her birthday, so he would have been talking to her a lot. At the time I convinced myself that she must have been in a relationship with him as well as with me – maybe just since the night in the hotel, or maybe from much longer before that. Who knows the truth? Whatever really happened, I felt like she had played me and made me feel a total fool. So that's when I went mad, and tweeted lots of things about Amy that people didn't understand at the time. I said, 'Everyone thinks Amy is a princess, but really she is a slut,' and things like that. It was harsh, but it's what I was feeling back then.

The problem with Amy is I think she did – maybe still does – love me. But she likes too many people, and falls in love easily. So do I, to be honest, and that is one of the reasons we get on. I can fall in love with a ham roll if it looks at me right! But I have looked at pictures of her and David since, and they do look happy and in love, so in one way I am pleased for her – at least I wasn't played for some guy who she broke up with a week later.

We haven't spoken since that day, and a part of me hates her for what she did. But I would still take her back, because we were so good together. In the end I know I would forgive her if she asked me to, because everything was so perfect with her, and I feel so good around her. I really did think she was the one, and that I would be married and have a kid with her by now. Even today, I am still in love with her.

So then I did what I always do when I am single because, as you know by now, I am not very good at being alone – I sat at home and started texting girls to cheer myself up. One of my friends is mates with Sarah Harding. I've always thought she was the fittest in Girls Aloud, and that she seemed sexy as hell, but also down to earth and friendly, despite being a celebrity. I was sure she was well out of my league – shit, I'm sure she could get anyone! – but I thought I'd give it a go. I'm never afraid of a knockback, so I said to my mate, 'Oi, set me up with her, will ya?' and he checked with her and she said he could give me her number, and we started texting. She was good banter on text, and after a bit I asked if she wanted to go on a date and she said yes, but that it would be too public if we went out so I should go round hers. Fuck! Sarah Harding was inviting me to her house.

So I went round and we watched a film and chilled and chatted and got to know each other. She was a really sweet, nice girl and she was just as down to earth as she seemed. She really opened up with me about her life, and I was touched that she felt so comfortable with me.

Then I went round a second time and we got on well again, but I also realized it was too soon after Amy for me to get into another relationship, and she deserved only the best, so in the end nothing happened. She is a genuinely lovely girl, and when she finds the right guy to settle down with, they are gonna find themselves with a gorgeous, fun and sexy girlfriend.

And I loved meeting her – that is something that would never have happened if I hadn't been famous. But it's funny dating someone when you're both well known. You can never go out and date the way you would normally. Things aren't allowed to progress in the same way. You have to keep everything secret and creep around, and most of the time to keep it private you go to each other's houses. I don't mind on one level, as all the wining and dining stuff has always made me feel awkward, like I said, but it does feel like proper relationships can never develop in a relaxed way.

I had a similar experience with another girl I have seen from time to time since late 2010 – Sheridan Smith. Apparently she used to fancy me and followed me on Twitter, but I didn't follow her so I never noticed her tweets. Then in November 2010 she started in *Legally Blonde* in the West End with Denise van Outen. Denise does the voice-over for *TOWIE* and so they came to Sugar Hut for a party after their first night performing. I got on with Sheridan straight away, and really liked her, but just as a mate. I was with Lauren at the time but I liked Sheridan as a normal, straight talking girl who is like one of the lads. I could leave her with my pals and she would be there chatting away. So nothing happened at the time, but we kept in touch. Then I went to watch her in *Legally Blonde* with two of my mates – imagine three straight lads off to watch that – and we had a few drinks together after and chilled out, and then, well, things have happened over time, whenever we have both been single and up for meeting.

I saw her a couple of weeks before the National TV Awards, then when I saw her at the ceremony itself on 22 January 2013 I felt like she practically blanked me. That has always done my nut in about her, that she seems to act like she doesn't really know me in public. Just before, I had been getting texts like, 'Hello, baby, how are you? I'm always thinking about you,' and that kind of thing.

I got to the awards and said, 'Hey, Sheridan!', all happy to see her.

'All right, Kirk,' she said, and she walked off.

How hard is it to have a conversation? I am sure that won't ruin your image! But there you go. She is a lovely girl, though, and she's someone who, in a different set-up, without fame getting in the way, I would have liked to have had a proper relationship with.

The one person my thoughts kept going back to was Gemma. She and Amy are still the only two girls who have properly got under my skin. I know people say you can only have one soul mate, but I think I have two. I love them both, but it doesn't look like I will ever end up with either one. Even when I had been with other girls after we'd split up, I would be thinking about Gemma. Not in a fantasy way, but in a 'Oh, Gemma would have done that differently,' or 'I miss how Gemma would do that,' kind of a way. I would even miss the way she kissed, which was the best kiss I've ever had in my life. But I knew I had fucked it up with her. There is no way she could forgive me yet again, and I kept going over and over everything I had said to her, really beating myself up about it.

My head was all over the place, and then in July 2012 I did a photoshoot with Jodie Marsh that I hugely regretted. Jodie had been a friend for a few years through Sugar Hut, where she was a regular, and although she had been a bit of a pin-up for me and most of the lads around Essex, nothing had ever happened between us.

When I had just split from Amy, Jodie was into all that bodybuilding, and I really didn't like the changes she was making to her body – I thought it didn't look good. But I admired her for trying to set up a business herself selling a nutritional range. So when she was looking to drum up a bit of publicity, I agreed to tweet a picture of us kissing, to help her out as a mate. Then we did a photoshoot to promote her range where we were pretty much naked, but it was so tacky and horrible that I hated it. Afterwards, all sorts of stories appeared in the papers saying that I had dumped her because she wouldn't have sex with me. We were never even dating! I just didn't need it. It was one thing to help her get some publicity, it was a totally different thing to be the fall guy for those kinds of stories! I went right off her after that, and we are no longer friends. To be honest I think she is a waste of space, so that is all the free publicity I even want to give her in this book!

Girls aside, everything else in my life was going from bad to worse. Things with Nan had been going downhill for a while. I used to go and visit her in the care home, but she never knew who I was. It was like it wasn't my nan any more, and so I stopped going to see her. Even when Mum had her out for weekends to stay with her, I couldn't face going round. That sounds horrible, but it was putting bad memories in my head, and I wanted to remember her as she was. Is it wrong to say I just wish she had died as she had been, so people could remember her like that?

I know some of my relatives thought I was bad not going to

see her, but I hope people can understand why I didn't. Obviously it wasn't that I didn't love her or I didn't care, but seeing her would have upset me so much that it was probably better for both of us that I stayed away.

Nan's time was up in July 2012, shortly after Amy and I split up, and I was gutted, but I knew in a way that because of the senile dementia we had really had lost her a long time before that.

At the same time, I wasn't getting on well with my dad. We had a falling out over some new girls he had hired to work in Sugar Hut, called Sugar Hut Honeys. The idea was that they were good looking girls who would be great promotion for the club, but the first time I saw them they were in bikinis. I went off on one, thinking that is how they would be dressed all the time and accusing Dad of making the club tacky. But the reality was that the bikinis were just for a photoshoot, and they are in dresses the rest of the nights. I had got the wrong end of the stick, but by the time I realized this it was too late – we'd already had the argument and there was bad feeling between us over it.

I also felt like Dad was enjoying the lifestyle that came with fame a bit too much. I would be home at night just watching a film, and I'd hear him get back late with a group of people and head for the hot tub. It just didn't seem right, and it was beginning to feel like I was the mature adult, and he was acting like a teenager!

To make things worse, I was still suffering from dark moments, getting anxious and depressed over nothing, thinking strangers in the street hated me. But this time my paranoia started expanding to include people close to me as well. I would wake up and feel down all day, for no reason, just thinking I had no mates and no one liked me. I'd sit and start deleting numbers from my phone, feeling there was no point in keeping them, when these people weren't my true friends.

Other times I would start the day off fine, and be walking down the road happy as Larry, when suddenly, for no reason, it was like a black cloud would come down over me, and I'd go home and cry.

It was the one thing I didn't feel like I could talk to my mum about. Maybe because I didn't understand what I was going through or why. I would have felt stupid saying, 'Hey, Mum, I reckon people hate me. No, I don't have a reason to say that or any proof, I just feel it.' But that is what I was feeling.

One of the big problems for me was – and still is, really – that I was stuck between two worlds. I am not from the same world as the rest of the people on TOWIE. I have not grown up knowing the nice lives that they have, where you don't have to fight for survival. I don't think I will ever fit into the moneyed world of people like them, and the other rich people I have met since becoming famous.

But on the other hand, I don't really fit into the world of the people I grew up with any more. I do have money, and it does set me aside. Plus the whole celebrity thing means they look at me differently. I might spend my evening on a red carpet at a premiere, and much as I'd like to take some of my Seabrooke Rise mates with me, they wouldn't fit in. It wouldn't work. So I don't fit perfectly with either group of friends. I am on my own, floating somewhere between the two. As I kept going over and over that in my mind, it would only add to my feeling of loneliness.

I had no girlfriend, no management – CAN obviously decided not to represent me after all when Amy split with me – no real mates (I believed), and no work, other than the odd bits I was still doing down at Sugar Hut. I really felt like things were falling apart for me.

I was totally lost and alone, and more paranoid and panicky than ever. I would spend hours going over and over my life, thinking about where things had gone wrong, trying to work out what I should have done differently.

One time I started watching bits of TOWIE back on YouTube, and I was watching my boxing fight with Mark. I started getting angry and stressed, and I guess my adrenalin was building and I could feel a panic attack coming on. I called Dad on his mobile, but he was in America and couldn't do much, except try to calm me down. But I was struggling to catch my breath, and it was making me worse, and I was saying, 'Dad, I can't breathe,' and that was it, I passed out, bang, on my floor. I came round a couple of minutes later, but I felt dizzy and panicked. It was the only time I actually passed out, but it was scary, and showed just how bad my anxiety was getting.

I was still being invited out to loads of places, and I'd go even though the people there weren't really my mates. Then when I was there I'd feel anxious and regret ever having left my house. So after a while I stopped going out at all, and would just sit in, chain-smoking, alone with my thoughts.

Mum didn't know what I was going through – I was still popping round to see her, but she would never really come to my house. It always felt too awkward, with Dad right next door, and as though I was rubbing our wealthy lifestyle in her face. So any time she questioned, 'Are you OK, Kirk? You don't seem like yourself, and you're not looking too well,' it was easy enough to brush it off as tiredness.

Dad didn't know what I was going through either, despite the fact that he lived next door. That is how little contact we were having with each other by then.

One person who did help me through it was my cousin Scott. He is eight years older than me, so we weren't close when we were younger. But by this time the age gap didn't matter, and he started coming round more. He understood me, and talked me through a lot of things, encouraging me to get back out there. He is big into the gym and started taking me down there with him, almost like he was my own personal trainer. He has become one of my best friends, and I owe him a lot for helping get me back on track.

Then at the end of summer 2012 my old manager Adam got back in touch to see if I wanted to give things another go. It suddenly sounded like he had ideas, and there were things out there that I could be doing with my life, instead of sitting around on my arse, spannering away my career.

He told me that TOWIE had a new producer, and the show was starting to introduce more of an open-door policy to past cast members. So whereas in the past anyone who chose to leave the show could never come back again, now there was a possibility people could return. This was exciting, as it did seem like they had been damaging themselves by blocking people from coming back – and I'm not big-headed enough just to be talking about me! So Adam suggested we approach them and see where things stood for me.

At the same time, although I didn't know it, my dad had been trying to get me back on the show. He knew there was something not quite right and was obviously worried about me.

When *TOWIE* said they did want me back, despite nine months away from the show, it gave me new energy to get myself on track mentally, and suddenly I felt inspired to believe in myself again. Filming for the seventh series began in September 2012, and I got stuck in – although I was nervous, I loved it. I much preferred *TOWIE* this time round under the new producer. People have accused the show of becoming less real, but actually I think the opposite is true. The new producers were trying to include much more of our real lives. For example, being able to acknowledge the fact that we are famous on the show has made it more realistic for viewers.

I also liked that I was able to tackle the whole issue of my anxiety and talk about it on the show, both with my fellow cast member Charlie King, and with the therapist Michael O'Doherty. I only saw the therapist once, as he lives in Ireland, but anyway I don't like to become dependent on other people. I only want to be reliant on myself. He made some good points, though, and suggested that being starved of oxygen when I was born could have caused my problems – that because I didn't have enough adrenalin then, when I needed it, my body has made up for it ever since by giving me too much whenever I feel like I'm in a bad situation.

Once I started to let people know about my anxiety, it became less of a big secret and I was able to relax a bit about it. I am suffering less at the moment, and I think that is why. I've had so many emails from people who suffer from anxiety, and it seems that I have really helped them by putting it out there in public on the show. People from fourteen to fifty years old who are going through the same thing have told me how pleased they are that I am addressing it.

I have found that there are pressure points that help as well, especially one on my wrist. It's the same place you would press to stop you being seasick, so you can even wear one of those travel bands. I've started wearing an elastic band on my wrist if I am going somewhere I think will be stressful, and if I ping it, it helps to reassure me, although I'm not sure why!

I'm even starting to do PAs again, as I don't feel so nervous about them. I have started using a technique where before I go on stage I imagine the worst thing that is going to happen. I treat it as fact that I am going to go out there and get booed, and called a prick, and all sorts. Then I breathe carefully and think, 'If that's the worst that can happen, I will deal with it.' And it is never that bad, so it is always easier than I have imagined it will be.

I know my personality is still as contradictory as ever. I can't say whether that's because I still don't fully know myself, or if everyone has two sides, and it is just more extreme in me. I can party like mad for a week and be Mr Sociable, then I'll sit in and tape every Jamie Oliver *30-Minute Meals* show, and spend a week cooking and getting them perfect. Not speaking to a single person, just making myself good at that. Then the next week I will be out partying again. Is that normal? I don't know. But it is me.

As for Lauren – well, we got it on again in series seven, although that hadn't been my plan! But when we had a barn dance and I saw her I realized I really wanted to talk to her, apologize for everything and check that she was doing OK – basically just have an adult conversation, and enjoy being in her company again. So after filming I said, 'Can we meet tomorrow and talk?' and I walked her down to her car by my front gate. I just felt really excited being with her and by the time I was saying goodbye I went in for a kiss, and it turned into a proper one. Then I turned round and saw the camera crew had spotted us and were filming, but we had been so caught up in each other, we hadn't even noticed.

When she got in she called me and we were on the phone for about an hour, just catching up and chatting about anything. We talked about getting back together, but both of us said that we shouldn't as there was a reason it hadn't worked the first time. But then the day after, she came over and we had sex. We both knew it was only sex, though. It was like we had missed it with each other, and that one day of sex got rid of any awkwardness between us, and we have been really close ever since.

Then the live show happened. Producers thought it would

be a good way to shake things up and prove to people how real and in the moment *TOWIE* actually is. It was based around an evening that Arg had organized, a charity showcase.

I offered to sing a cover of Dean Martin's hit song 'Ain't That A Kick In The Head?', and I was so scared. If I hadn't been sitting down on a chair on stage, I would have fallen over. I didn't know what I was doing at all, and I completely messed up my words, but I carried on, and I was really proud of myself for that. I think the adrenalin that normally kicks in when I panic worked in the right way this time, and kept me going and enjoying it on some level, rather than wanting to run off the stage and collapse!

The hardest bit that night must have been the conversation between Joey and Sam about their future. It was so awkward, and such a private conversation to be having in front of a million viewers. I felt bad for Joey, and could see him crumbling, but was glad that it was him this time, and not me and Lauren!

The high point for me, though, was when Lauren was talking about having sex with me. She said I had always been good, but had got even better. I got some serious man points for that!

As for women, there has been no one special in my life for a good while. But there was one famous singer who got right inside my head, and who made me really curious about her, then bang, she disappeared . . . That lady was Rita Ora.

On Twitter in the autumn I wrote a list of my top five hottest women in the world, and she was in the number one slot. I've always been a massive fan of both her music and her looks.

Next thing I knew she was following me! So I took the plunge, thought, 'Fuck it, nothing to lose,' and I private messaged her. And she messaged back, and we kept chatting. Nothing too full on, just a bit of flirting.

Then I was at the O2 in London doing a gig and met her backstage. She was being pulled through, but stopped for a minute to say 'hi' and she grabbed my arms and said, 'Cor, you are big,' winked, and was on her way.

It was all so surreal, but I decided to move it up a level, so I sent her my number. A few days later I was in bed and got a missed call from a number that I didn't recognize. I texted, 'Who is this?'

And got a reply: 'Answer the phone next time and you will find out.'

So of course I did, and it was her. I was like, 'Are you messing? I'm actually talking to Rita Ora!'

And that was it. She called me all the time, and we would chat for ages, and had really good banter and were flirting loads. I had seen in the papers that she was supposed to be dating Rob Kardashian, but she made a real point of telling me she didn't have a boyfriend.

Then she phoned me as she was on her way to the MTV EMA awards in Frankfurt where she was going to perform, and talked to me right until she was on the plane and the phone cut out. Then she called as soon as she landed in Germany and said, 'I actually really like you, despite us only talking on the phone. Why don't you fly out to Frankfurt and join me?'

And I sat there in total panic, thinking, 'Do I, don't I? I really want to, that is any man's dream! But does that make me look desperate?!' So in the end I said I couldn't, but would love to see her when she was back in the UK.

And she said, 'Fine, I'll be back in a week. It will be too mad if we go out, but how about you come round mine and watch a film the day after I'm home?'

I couldn't believe it was happening! And we kept talking right until she was heading back to London, and she said she would text me when she landed. Then, no word. She had been so on it I even had a moment of thinking her plane had crashed – what other explanation could there be?!

So then, well, I guess I pestered her for a couple of weeks, because I didn't understand what had happened, texting and messaging her on Twitter. Until eventually I just said, 'You are messing with my head, no idea what is happening, but I give up!'

And she replied, 'I'm sorry, but there is a lot coming up for me at the moment, I can't really talk.'

And then a couple of days later all the stories came out in the paper about her breaking up with Rob, and him tweeting, accusing her of sleeping with twenty guys while she was with him. Maybe if the timing had been better, I would have been guy number twenty-one!

I think she is a great girl, and would still go on that date in a heartbeat. She still follows me on Twitter, so you never know . . .

FOURTEEN

The Future

As for the future, well, I'm not too sure which way I am headed. I have become mates with Danny Dyer, who I have always thought was an incredible actor. Not only that, but we are very similar. I look at him and see someone with a past very much like mine, and I see him as me in ten years' time, with more knowledge of himself and understanding of the world. He has become like an older brother to me, and I think he sees himself in me too.

Danny has been encouraging me to give acting a go, and I recently tried out for a film role to star alongside him, which would be amazing. I got really positive feedback from the producers, so fingers crossed for that.

I am also looking at designing my own clothing range and have begun gathering together ideas for that. I love fashion and clothes, so I think it would be something really good to get involved in. I am really into visual stuff, so I think I could come up with a great range for men. When it comes to any maths or measurements, though, I will be sure to leave that to the actual designers!

Most of all, though, I want to give singing a go. I think I proved on the live episode of *TOWIE* that I have a decent voice, and I want to release a single sometime this year and see what kind of response it gets. I want people to judge me as a completely new singer, rather than someone who is famous and trying to record off the back of it. I think I can prove myself the hard way, and succeed. Dappy has put me in touch with some useful people and if I can make that my plan for the year, I'll be happy. I'm an entertainer, and I want to make people smile!

While I have been finishing the book, series eight of *TOWIE* has been on television. It started off well, and was fun to film at first. I liked being reunited with Joey, and 'Team Jirk' making its return! And I was up for sticking with the show for the next while, because the only way for me really is Essex – whether it's Brentwood or Grays.

But then things started getting weird and all these doubts kicked in. I was shocked when I thought that Lauren might be pregnant by me. It was a head fuck! Even though I knew that the test was negative by the time the show went out, watching it on my sofa with my mum was awful. That whole episode proper messed with my head. Although it just turned out to be a scare, I was asking myself if being on *TOWIE* was worth the mess that was going on in my head.

Then it felt – and this sounds like an odd thing to complain about, I know – that I was being made into too much of the show's pin-up. It felt like I was being filmed with my top off in every scene. Gym scenes, shower scenes, even at home on the phone. Don't get me wrong, it was great on one level! But it made me think, is this all I've got to offer? There was a lot else going on in my life that they could have filmed, like me having a laugh with Joey, and looking for a new girlfriend. But for whatever reason they didn't.

Then Dad quit the show. He had begun to think Sugar Hut wasn't coming across the way he wanted, and he thought it had gone as far as it could on air. TOWIE was great for giving the club a boost when it was needed in the beginning, but he wants to show everyone that Sugar Hut is a good club in itself – not just because it's on TV – and he feels that now is the right time to do it. From what I have seen so far, he is really happy with his decision. But, although it may be a coincidence, when he left the show it felt like I was in it less too.

Plus outside of the show, all my friends were telling me they thought it was time to quit. They said, 'You should leave while there are lots of other options out there.' Danny was telling me the same, and so was my dad, who could see I wasn't happy.

For me, a major thing that was going wrong was that the show wasn't focusing on the right kind of people. TOWIE used to be about kids who were at least trying to be success- ful – opening their own businesses, trying to get on in life and follow their dreams. But it seemed as if it was beginning to focus on people who had no jobs, who were just spending all day messing around. It wasn't my reality, so it felt wrong for me to be a part of it.

So I sat down and had a serious think about it all. I went over everything that I had a problem with, and thought about what would happen if I stayed or if I left. And well, my conclusion was: I quit.

It wasn't an easy decision, as even when I hadn't liked previous storylines or had struggled with the fame it had brought, I really can say I have loved my time on the show. It has opened some amazing doors for me. But I think I have done the right thing by leaving, and now I am excited about what lies in the future for me.

Writing this book, I have realized just how weird my life has been. I would never change it, though, because it has made me who I am now. I just wish I had understood some of the things I was going through a bit better at the time. But today I have a bit more faith in myself to get things right. I've made enough mistakes that hopefully I am learning!

As for girls . . . well, I've always known I love them! But writing this has made me realize a few things about the way I behave with them. The closer they are to me the meaner I seem to be to them. I don't know if that is because I'm afraid of losing someone again, the way I lost my dad, so I reject them before they can reject me. That is just a theory. But I can see that I have definitely done this a few times, especially with Gemma. She is the one girl who I have obsessed about again and again, and who I know I totally messed things up with. I'd be so happy if I could apologize and give things another go. I just don't know if she can get past the way I have behaved, and if not, well, I hope I have learned my lesson for the next amazing girl who comes along.

One thing I do know is that I can't wait to be a parent. That is my absolute dream, and I hope I don't have to wait too long. But I know from having watched my parents that it is no easy job. You can do your best not to fuck it up, and I'm sure no parent sets out to make mistakes, but they do happen, and we are all human.

My mum was – and is – the absolute best mum in the world. She grafted so hard and did everything she could to make me happy and have the best life possible. And now I need to repay her the best I can. It breaks my heart that she is still living in a shit little flat, while I'm in an amazing house. But she was ill again last year and had to stop work for a while, and it feels like she has endless bad luck. I go round and give her money to help out, but I want to make a real difference to her life. If I can buy her a flat of her own in a nice area in the next year or so, then I will be happy.

As for Dad, well, he wasn't around while we were growing up, and no matter what he thinks about that, it was a shame. Daniel and I missed out, but then I think so did he. I know he had his reasons, though, and I understand them better now I am older. And once we got to eighteen, he definitely did his best to make up for lost time. But still, to this day, I don't know for sure if he loves me because he has to, or if he loves me for me. It would be nice to hear it from him once and for all. But at least I have him, and I hope I have a great relationship with him for the rest of my life.

Mum made me the nice young boy I could be, and still can be. She is the one who taught me about being a good human being. Dad is the one who taught me to be an adult. Through tough love he made me the man I am today. And I think I needed both of them. I know that growing where I did, living in a family where everything was nice and perfect wouldn't have prepared me for the outside world. I had to fight to survive as a kid, and maybe the problems I was dealing with in my family taught me how to do that. Maybe things happened exactly the way they were supposed to.

I don't think people really know the Essex I've experienced, and I do want everyone who I've grown up with to understand that I've not forgotten my roots. It made me who I am today. Not made me a doughnut or a prick or an arrogant idiot. That's why when people look at me and say, 'You're flash,' I can answer, hand on heart, 'I ain't flash, man, I'm thankful.'

Acknowledgements

Mum, obviously my first and biggest thank you goes to you. Thanks for always believing in me no matter what, and supporting me through absolutely everything in life. You taught me that life is not all about money, but about making a difference. Love you.

Dad, thank you for rescuing me when you did, and teaching me to be tough, or I'd never have survived through my childhood. You have become one of my best mates, and I hope it stays that way.

Daniel, thanks for beating the shit out of me over the years, and being exactly how an older brother should be!

Dappy, thank you for teaching me to be humble, and for being a great friend, always there when I need a chat.

Danny, you are my right-hand man and the best raver I know. A party is not a party without you there!

Scott, thank you for being a friend as well as a cousin – and for keeping me on a strict diet and in shape!

My manager Adam, thank you for putting the time and effort into me, and being on hand with advice and a trip to Essex to see me whenever I have needed it.

Emma Donnan, thank you for your help putting my story into words – it has been an emotional ride and you were the perfect person to go through that with.

Ingrid Connell and all at Pan Macmillan, thank you for giving me the chance to tell my story, and for being great to work with. And Andrew Lownie, thank you for helping set up the deal in the first place.

AM Concepts UK, thank you, including Ian Minton, for all your hard work.

Thanks to Dave Almond and Ian Stoddart from Peace Of Mind for looking after me when I am on the road.

My Lime Pictures family past and present – Amanda Murphy, Kate Little, Sean Murphy, Ruth Wrigley and Tony Wood – thank you.

Thanks to TOWIE for giving me the wings so I could go out and fly. Hopefully this is just the beginning.

To all my fans, especially on twitter (@kirk_official) thank you for the support and the banter, let's keep it going and thank you for buying my book!

Picture Acknowledgements

All photographs are from the author's private collection apart from:

Page 1: © ITV/Rex Features

Page 8 top and bottom: © ITV/Rex Features

Page 9: top left © ITV/Rex Features; top right: ©XPOSUREPHOTOS.COM

Bottom left: photograph by Harleymoon Kemp,

© Matrix Studios/AM Concepts UK

Page 10 top: ©XPOSUREPHOTOS.COM

Page 11 top: ©XPOSUREPHOTOS.COM;

bottom right ©Mark Milan/FilmMagic

Page 12 bottom: © Richard Barker/Rex Features